CHOSEN

CHOSEN
KNOW YOUR KINGDOM ASSIGNMENT

KELLIE LANE

authorHOUSE®

AuthorHouse™
1663 Liberty Drive
Bloomington, IN 47403
www.authorhouse.com
Phone: 1-800-839-8640

Published by AuthorHouse 7/16/2014

ISBN: 978-1-4969-1892-5 (sc)
ISBN: 978-1-4969-1893-2 (e)

Unless noted, all scripture is from KJV.

Chosen
/CHōzən/

[1]   Having been selected as the best or most appropriate [1]

I dedicate this book to my sisters in Christ, Molisha and Tomeikla. They have been there for me through thick and thin, forever present with a word of encouragement. They believed in me when I didn't have the faith to believe in myself. So to my sisters, thank you for revealing to me that God could actually take my messed-up life and turn it into something beautiful. You two encouraged me to write even when I felt that no one else in the world would have any interest in anything that I had to say. You both helped me to realize that I do have a purpose, and that purpose shall be fulfilled. God bless you.

ACKNOWLEDGMENTS

I would like to take this opportunity to acknowledge my husband, Lavon. Honey, thank you for putting up with me. My heart is filled with gratitude. You are the answer to my prayers.

I would like to blow kisses to my children, Chrystian, Kailey, Micah, Khloe, Lakyn, and Lathyn. You six are my heartbeat.

My heart says thank you to the Word of Life Church family. Pastor Joel, your powerful messages gave me the insight needed to complete this work.

I would like to acknowledge my sister, Shannell. Shannell, when we lost Mom, we gained each other. Thank you for being my best friend.

Special thanks to the Nu Vision Worship Center International Church family. I love you all so much. Pastor Richardson and Prophetess Richardson, what would I do without your guidance? May God continuously bless you, and may his countenance shine upon you.

Many blessings to the Spring Hill Christian Center Church family. Dr. Williams, thank you for opening your doors to me over and over again. There is no place like home.

Last but certainly not least, I would like to recognize my mother, Chiquita Marie. Mama, I know you are one proud lady looking down on me from heaven.

WHY I WROTE THIS BOOK

There is nothing that I write about that I do not first painfully live out. I once heard Bishop T. D. Jakes say that until you go through a particular thing, you are not qualified to be heard. It makes perfect sense to me. There are so many people out there who feel the same way that I felt when I first began my journey of self-discovery. I repeatedly cried out to God, "Why am I here? What did you task me to do?" I was tired of feeling as if something was missing from my life. I had the career, I had a decent social life, I had family, and I had a relationship with God, yet my heart was yearning for more. What I had to realize was that the sense of discontentment was real. My heart had been programmed by God for a greater cause, and I could no longer settle for staying where I was. I tried to convince myself that I was not good enough to be used by God. I'm sure that he could've easily handpicked someone else with a better track record. But he didn't. God was well aware of my flaws, yet he still chose me. Friend, the enemy wants to convince us that we are not good enough, or smart enough, or rich enough, or talented enough to do a great work for the kingdom. Yet we know that the devil is a liar. As a matter of fact, he is the father of lies. You must immediately reject anything that he plants into your heart. I am a living testimony that God will take you as you are and turn around every situation in your life for his Glory. He has chosen you to be his ambassador.

CONTENTS

FOREWORD

Christian Calling

O Lord God,
The first act of calling is by Thy
command in the Word,
"Come unto Me, return unto Me."
—Arthur Bennet[1]

When I read this prayer called "Christian Calling" from the book *The Valley of Vision*[1], I instantly began constructing a series of questions. First, in this effectual calling, who is actually doing this sovereign choosing for the greater good in my life? Is it actually me, or is it our eternal and invisible God who chooses? Second, if it is God, why is this calling significant for me right now—especially in the midst of the trials, tribulations, and difficulties of life—when I am able to make decisions for myself?

Chosen, by my wife, Dr. Kellie Lane, is a thought-provoking and Spirit-led book resulting from her submission to the Lord and savior, Christ Jesus, and God. I have the great pleasure of offering a small, humble, and valuable critique of her experience in profoundly engaging in and comprehending the luxury of being God's chosen one.

Initially, Kellie directed us to a mind-blowing place in her first book, *When God Is Silent,* allowing the readers (including myself as her husband) to dive into the deepest, finest, and most sacred places of her life, where all of her resources and energy were depleted in devotion to God. Yet he (still) gave the impression of—or at least it was perceived as—silence. Now, after truly having the spiritual scales removed from her eyes, along with a heart of flesh (Acts 9:18; Ezekiel 36:26), Kellie passionately explains and exploits the manifestation of the divine election. She shares for the brethren and the lost how to get godly wisdom and understanding as it equates to sovereign choosing through the Word of God (Proverbs 16:16) for the sake of your life and soul here on earth and hereafter in the eternal state.

God calls out his own, equips them with the Word, and then they, in turn, preach the Gospel to others. From here, the elect will be called out. Kellie is building a case to help you understand, as the reader, hearer, and doer, what it means to be chosen by God. Therefore, the overall diagnosis is broken down as such: in Luke 9:35, God the Father chooses; in John 13:1–20, God the Son chooses; and in 2 Thessalonians 2:13–17, we are chosen through sanctification by God the Holy Spirit.

Lastly, in all humility, I thank my wife, Kellie, for her blessings in allowing me to give my thoughts on a very tough subject in order to draw closer to the personhood of our triune God and his work for our salvation.

"So that we may put on kindness, humility, meekness, and patience, bearing with one another, forgiving each other as The Lord has forgiven you who called have been called in one body where Christ rules in your hearts and dwells richly" (Colossians 3:12–17).

In Christ alone,
 Lavon Lane

INTRODUCTION

*Ye have not chosen me, but I have chosen you, and
ordained you, that ye should go and bring forth fruit,
and that your fruit should remain: that whatsoever ye
shall ask of the Father in my name, he may give it you.*
—John 15:16

Do you know what it really means to be chosen by
God? *Webster*[1] defines chosen as "one who is the object
of choice or of divine favor: an elect person." God made
you his choice. You are the elect. You were specifically
handpicked by God, even before the foundations of the
earth were created, to do a great work for his kingdom.
You were in the mind of God before your father ever
met your mother. It doesn't matter who your mother
is or who your father is. You may have been given up
for adoption. You may have been a result of incest or
rape. Yet, you are still chosen. You are the creation,
and God is the creator. Your purpose is to be here. The
circumstances surrounding your birth have no bearing
on your assignment in the kingdom. It doesn't matter
where you are now. It doesn't matter what others said you

would become. For whatever reason, God handpicked you for a unique task. More than likely, you are not qualified and have no idea how or why God would even choose you. Yet he did. You didn't choose him; he chose you. Remember that.

I once worked for an employer who repeatedly preselected individuals for hire. The cycle would repeat itself over and over. A new position would post and immediately you would hear rumors regarding who the position actually belonged to. Now I'm not too fond of the rumor mill, yet time after time, what was said actually came to pass. It became apparent that someone who had insight was leaking information. Human resources considered this practice illegal. Yet it happened repeatedly. It angered me so much because it really didn't give other potentially qualified candidates a fair chance. The application process was often very lengthy and required a bit of running around. Yet for most of those who applied, it was all in vain. The verdict was out before the case was even presented.

As I began to write this book, God reminded me of the similarities between what was happening on that job and how things operate in the kingdom. Being chosen by God means you have been preselected for God's position. No one else can take it from you. It's yours and it uniquely fits you. You are the most qualified. There's no tedious application process to be completed in vain. You don't have to worry about whether or not you will answer the questions just right because there is no interview panel checking off grading sheets or crossing you off a list as you proceed. Even if someone else desires your position, they can't have it. God tailored it just for you. At my previous workplace, there were other qualified individuals who could've done the job right had they been given a chance. With God, however, you are the only one who can get the job done. Take comfort in knowing that.

So how do you know if you've been chosen? If you were not chosen, you would not ask that question. It's just that simple. You have come to a place in your life where you are beginning to feel a sense of urgency. God placed that feeling in your heart so that you will begin to look inward. You will begin to seek God like never before. You need answers. Like a fish out of water, you are feeling as if you will soon suffocate if there is no change in your current situation. You must realize the power of God. He is your source. He is your friend. If you remain in constant fellowship with him, you can rest assured that his will for your life will be revealed. It's not rocket science. God placed you here for a reason and wants to reveal that reason to you. May the word of God fill your mouth as his purpose for you fills your heart.

But as it is written, "Eye hath not seen, nor ear heard, neither have entered into the heart of man, the things which God hath prepared for them that love him" (1 Corinthian 2:9).

God loves you so much. You must take some time and really let that sink in. He only wants the best for your life. You are constantly on his mind. Nothing pleases him more than to be in constant fellowship with you. You are the center of his joy. You are his baby. He will answer your prayers in the middle of the night. He will step over others to get to you. You must get this into your head. No more self-defeating thoughts. No more depression. No more frustration. We will bind those spirits right now. God is with you. He's on your side. You are not alone. Tell yourself, "I am chosen." You have open access to the kingdom of God.

Draw a line in the sand and tell the devil, "Enough is enough!" The time has come for heaven and earth to kiss on your behalf. Everything that has been misaligned must come into divine alignment now. No more setbacks. It's time for the comeback. Legions of angels have been assigned to you to ensure that your mission is accomplished. You are protected. No devil in hell can stop what God has ordained.

If your heart has led you to pick up this book, it is because God is calling you to something greater. You have a mission. You don't have to be perfect. Trust me, I am far from that. All you have to be is willing.

It is my prayer that this book will be a source of strength for you. You will be inspired as you journey through its pages. No matter the opposition, know that you can do it. You are the missing piece to the world's puzzle. Your life has purpose. Repeat after me: "My life has purpose." You deserve only the best. Reach for it now in the mighty name of Jesus. Be blessed.

CHAPTER ONE

Be Yourself

To be beautiful means to be yourself. You don't need to be accepted by others. You need to accept yourself.
—Thich Nhat Hanh[1]

For many years, I was not happy with who I was. No matter what I did, I could not find satisfaction within myself. I didn't like my lips. I thought they were too full. Why? Because all I can remember growing up was being told that I had a big mouth. I hated my size. I was short and chubby growing up and was teased a lot. So, all of my life, I've been weight conscious. To make matters worse, as a young girl, I was often compared to my older sister. She was extremely beautiful, and I, on the other hand, was considered the ugly duckling. She had long, dark, silky hair. My hair was a dusty brown color, kinky, and very difficult to manage. She could sing like an angel, yet I could barely hold a tune. I would always think to myself, *If only I had long, beautiful hair like my sister. If only I could sing like my sister. If only I could be beautiful like my sister.*

My family would always tell me that I may not look like my sister or have hair like her or be able to sing like her, but, "Remember, Kellie, you're smart." I was instructed to focus on my intelligence. So that's exactly what I did. I considered myself ugly but smart. I made up my mind at a very young age to be the best that I could be at whatever I put my mind to. I remember from the day I picked up a clarinet to the day I put it down, I was first chair. In all of my classes, I had to make an A. I had to be the best at everything that I did, and honestly, in some instances, I am still that way. But what was my driving force? What God allowed me to realize many years later was the *why* behind the *what*. There was a reason I pushed myself so hard. There was a reason I was never satisfied with the length of my own hair or the size of my lips. I was subconsciously trying to be someone else. I didn't realize that God made me beautiful too. Yes, I was different from my sister, yet I was equally beautiful. God placed what he wanted to place on the inside of her. He also placed what he wanted to place on the inside of me. Her gifts and attributes are no better than mine. We're just different. We're two different people with two different assignments, but all in all, we were both put here on earth to glorify God and to add value to his people.

> And he gave some, apostles; and some, prophets; and some, evangelists; and some, pastors and teachers; For the perfecting of the saints, for the work

of the ministry, for the edifying of the
body of Christ: Till we all come in the
unity of the faith, and of the knowledge
of the Son of God, unto a perfect man,
unto the measure of the stature of the
fulness of Christ: That we henceforth
be no more children, tossed to and fro,
and carried about with every wind of
doctrine, by the sleight of men, and
cunning craftiness, whereby they lie in
wait to deceive; But speaking the truth
in love, may grow up into him in all
things, which is the head, even Christ:
From whom the whole body fitly joined
together and compacted by that which
every joint supplieth, according to the
effectual working in the measure of
every part, maketh increase of the body
unto the edifying of itself in love.

(Ephesians 4:11–16)

The scriptures clearly teach us that God uniquely
gifted each of us. If he wanted everyone to be a pastor,
he would've called us all to pastor. If he wanted everyone
to have the ability to sing, he would've made us all
songbirds. If he wanted us all to look alike, he could've
easily done that. But he chose not to. So what am I
saying? We must learn to appreciate our differences
instead of trying to be more like someone else. When
we do not accept ourselves, it's as if we are telling God

that he didn't make us good enough. All in all, our ultimate purpose as a people is to join together, bringing our gifts and talents forward so that the body of Christ can receive increase.

I remember the day that I allowed my hair to return to its natural state. I went to the local barber and asked her to cut all of the straight ends off. My hair had been subject to chemical treatments since I was about ten years of age. As I watched my hair hit the floor, I took a deep sigh of relief. I looked at myself in the mirror. My hair was maybe four inches long and kinky, and there was that dusty brown color that I remembered so well from my childhood. I'd been dying my hair and processing it for so long that I'd almost forgotten its real color and texture. I was so proud of myself. It was more than just allowing my hair to return to its natural state. For me, it was an outward expression of me finally accepting myself. It didn't matter that my hair didn't turn into beautiful curly locks or that my lips and nose actually were more noticeable now with all of the hair gone. I didn't care. I was totally satisfied. For once in my life, I was satisfied with Kellie. It no longer mattered that I didn't look like my sister. It didn't matter that I couldn't sing like her. It didn't matter that my lips are fuller than hers.

One of my closest friends later asked me, "Kellie, how long are you going to wear your hair like this, because this is not you." She couldn't believe that I was comfortable wearing very short, unprocessed hair. It was so different from how she'd ever seen me.

I smiled and told her, "I'm not sure. If I decide to change it, I will, but for now I'm content just the way that I am."

So what am I saying here? I believe before you can truly do a great work for God, you have to be at peace with yourself. We may each have different circumstances. Yet we must learn to accept who we really are and be comfortable with that person and love that person no matter what. For years, I thought that I was content when I actually wasn't. I was always trying to make adjustments to my appearance. There is nothing wrong with doing what makes you feel good. Just be sure that you are doing it for the right reason.

We must understand that according to man's standards, we may not look like someone else or have the genetic build of someone else, yet God created us in his image and likeness. How much more perfect can it get? Please understand that you are fearfully and wonderfully made:

"I will praise thee; for I am fearfully and wonderfully made: marvellous are thy works; and that my soul knoweth right well" (Psalm 139:14).

God created the Psalmist, as well as every one of us, in a wonderful way and for a specific purpose. When we truly understand that, we can feel peace, knowing that whatever weaknesses or perceived problems we have in life are there because God ordained them. Take comfort in knowing that God has created you the way you are for a reason. You don't have to feel undue pressure to be like other people, because God purposely did not make you like other people.

We must be thankful and honor Jehovah, God, for the body and life that he has given us. God does not randomly drop people into this world without considering their needs and situations. God knows the very number of hairs on our heads (Luke 12:7). God loves us so much. In return, we must be forever grateful for the life and body he has graced us with. You don't have to change a thing about yourself. God made you for his glory. He placed you on the potter's wheel and formed you until he saw that what he created was good. He decided your eye color, your hair texture and length, and your ethnicity. He gave you your grandma's big nose and your daddy's green lookers. Be happy with it! He also gifted you in a way that brings pleasure to him. If you have the ability to sing, sing for Jesus! Figure out how to use that gift for his glory alone. If you have the gift of writing, sewing, drawing, dancing, whatever it may be, think about what you are doing with the gift. Whatever it is that God has given you, get busy with it. I charge you to be all about your father's business.

The Bible says God formed you.

Thus saith the Lord, thy redeemer, and he that formed thee from the womb, I am the Lord that maketh all things; that stretcheth forth the heavens alone; that spreadeth abroad the earth by myself.

(Isaiah 44:24)

Not only did God form each of us, but he also considers us his workmanship and considers us his very own masterpieces.

For we are his workmanship, created in Christ Jesus unto good works, which God hath before ordained that we should walk in them.

(Ephesians 2:10)

So what's the take-home message? Regardless of the situation, please learn to be content with the way that God has gloriously made you. You do not have to be like anyone else. It's perfectly OK to be you. Realize your worth today so that God's peace may come upon you and his purpose for your life may be fulfilled.

Let us pray:

Father God, we humbly thank you for creating us in the image and likeness of you. We now realize what it means to be fearfully and wonderfully made. Grace us, Lord, with the ability to truly love and accept ourselves. In Jesus's name. Amen.

CHAPTER TWO

Forgive Yourself

How unhappy is he who cannot forgive himself.
—Publilius Syrus[1]

I think that the hardest thing that I've ever done in my life was to forgive myself for the series of failed relationships and marriages that I once repeatedly involved myself in. Perhaps I am the only one who has struggled with forgiving myself and others so I'll just focus on me and my issues for a moment. It was as if I'd been plagued. Every person who I thought was Mr. Right ended up being Mr. Dead Wrong. Did I ignore the signs? Was I that desperate for love? How could I think that a man who didn't love God could love me? That's the first big red flag. I know that this is not a relationship book, but I have to switch gears for just a moment.

Disclaimer: Do not involve yourself with anyone who does not put God first. If you do, you're headed toward destruction.

If that person does not love God, how in the world do you think that he or she will ever love you? The answer is they can't. So hopefully I saved at least one person a little heartache and pain, or maybe even ten years of being involved in fruitless relationships. You see, I'm not perfect, nor do I profess to be. I tried to love people who had no clue how to love me. Love does not blacken your eyes, love does not spit in your face, and love does not cheat on you. Love does not get angry when you attend church. Love does not sit on the couch and do nothing while you go to work every day. Love does not come into your home all times of the night. That's not the love that the Apostle Paul speaks about in the Book of Corinthians. I pray that I'm helping somebody right now.

We all know the love chapter in the Book of Corinthians:

Charity suffereth long, and is kind; charity envieth not; charity vaunteth not itself, is not puffed up, Doth not behave itself unseemly, seeketh not her own, is not easily provoked, thinketh no evil; Rejoiceth not in iniquity, but rejoiceth in the truth; Beareth all things, believeth all things, hopeth all things, endureth all things.

(1 Corinthians 13:4–7)

So why do we settle for less than God's best? I remember how I used to beat myself up about my terrible track record. I would ask myself, "Why can't I be like normal people? Why can't I connect with a God-fearing man who would willingly love me as Jesus Christ loves and adores the church?" Why couldn't I just get married once and stay married for like sixty years? Was that too much to ask? Well, actually, it's not too much to ask of God. What I later realized is that I did not seek the face of God before I jumped into unfavorable situations that later harmed me. I missed the mark over and over. I'm being real with you because I am trying to help you. I need you to realize that God does not choose perfect people. He uses those with imperfections. In my case, he chose to use someone with more imperfections than one can count.

For years, I tried to bury my past, and believe it or not, it worked for a while. I didn't want anyone to know what a mess I'd made of my life. I had it seemingly all together in most areas, but when it came down to relationships, two words describe it best: train wreck. Yet, all along, I had a strange feeling that one day God was going to force me to spill the beans. He was going to use me to encourage others with the very thing that I was trying so desperately to hide. Remember David in the Bible? Back in those times, two of the ultimate no-no's of sin were to commit murder or adultery. And guess what? David managed to commit them both. Did God not still use him in a mighty way? Yes, he did. David was known as a man after God's own heart.

Friend, your issue may not be relationships or it very well may be. It may be a drug or alcohol addiction. You may be addicted to sex. You may have a lying spirit. Whatever it is, know that it's time for you to be healed, restored, and set free once and for all. You may think that you are delivered already. But, if you still feel ashamed to talk about it you're not quite there yet. Part of that process requires you to forgive yourself. It's okay. You have no idea how your experience can set the captives free. God knows that. Why do you think he chose you? God knew what you were going to do before he formed the foundations of the earth. Even then, you were predestined to do a great work for the kingdom.

The Bible teaches us that the rain falls on the just and the unjust alike. In other words, we all go through things. We all have times of difficulty. What we have to truly understand is that no matter what, God can still make our lives beautiful. We've all made some decisions that we are not so proud of. Every one of us has missed the mark in one way or another. You can't live the rest of your life wearing a scarlet letter because you made an imperfect decision. God has forgiven you if you asked for it. Now you must forgive yourself. This is why it is critical for each of us to have a personal relationship with our creator. The more we come into the knowledge of him, the more accepting of ourselves we will become. Regardless of your issue, there is nothing so grand that you cannot move past it. There's nothing in your past that can disqualify you for what God has for you now. He can still get the glory, no matter the situation. God can give you his beauty for your ashes. Let's take a look at it in scripture:

To appoint unto them that mourn in Zion, to give unto them beauty for ashes, the oil of joy for mourning, the garment of praise for the spirit of heaviness; that they might be called trees of righteousness, the planting of the LORD, that he might be glorified.

(Isaiah 61:3)

In Biblical times, it was the custom for the people of that day to lie in ashes during great times of mourning and difficulty. If this was still the custom of today, I wonder how many of us would be hanging out in ash piles. God declares in his word that all who mourn in Zion (those who dwell in the house of God) will be given beauty for ashes. Now what exactly does that mean? It means that God will take our mess—the things in our lives that we consider embarrassing, disgusting, shameful, and downright horrible—and exchange all of that for something beautiful. No matter how ugly things may seem right now, all can be made beautiful under the right conditions. In many ways, our lives can be compared to that of the American aloe. Ever heard of it?

The American aloe, also known as the century plant[2], has a stem that is hard and bulky. It has elongated, fleshy leaves with spiny margins that can potentially reach lengths of six feet or more. Each leaf has a heavy spike at the tip that is sharp enough to pierce to the bone. The longer the plant lives, the more calloused it becomes. It grows this way for years and years, but then all of a sudden, when it reaches its full maturity, a thick stalk as tall as twenty feet shoots up through the middle of the plant. Next, thousands of beautiful yellow flowers sprout out all at once and the American aloe becomes a beautiful, unique plant.

Like the American aloe, we too can become calloused if we're not careful. We can become smothered in layers and layers of regret, heartache, and disappointment. We can lose sight of our dreams and visions. This is a trap. Don't fall for it! This is exactly what the enemy wants. The devil would much rather you waddle around in modern day ash piles than decide to be an overcomer for Christ. If he can steal your focus he wins.

Perhaps at one point you had really big dreams but somehow they've faded away. Perhaps you once had the desire to do a great work for the Lord, but somehow you got off course. Do you realize that you can dream again, regardless of the situation? As a matter of fact, you must dream again! Yes, it can come to pass. You're not going crazy. God is ready to make your life beautiful. He is ready to wow all of those around you who swore you would never amount to anything. He will shush the mouths of every person who spoke ill against what you believed in. Trust me. I am a living witness. It's not over, friend. As a matter of fact, this is only the beginning. I am so excited for you!

Listen, we all have traveled down some difficult roads throughout our lifetime. At times, we've even taken a wrong turn. Yes, we've made some bad decisions. Yes, we've missed the mark in one area or another. We may have even ignored the warning signs. But now what? Can we can back up and fix it? Should we kick, scream, and cry over things that happened in yesteryear? No, we mustn't. Yesteryear is gone forever. Make a decision to leap forward. Propel yourself into greatness. It awaits you. You are not so big of a sinner that God cannot totally transform your life. But you must be willing. *Willing to do what, Kellie?* I'm glad you asked.

You must be willing to lay aside every weight and sin that easily besets you (Hebrews 12:1). There's no room for junk in your new season. It's time to trust the author and finisher of your faith with your whole heart (Hebrews 12:2). No more doing things your own way. Besides, how did that benefit you? Move past your failures. Rise up out of your ashes. Confuse the enemy! Satan knew for sure that your life was toast. Prove him wrong. You must break free. Your time for total transformation has come. Embrace it. You will look back and say, "Wow. I never thought that my life could be so beautiful." There won't even be a trace of what used to be. What a mighty God we serve. He is one who willingly washes all of our sins away. He is a father who wants his children to have only the best. Now that is worth celebrating. You have the victory. You just have to believe it. No more excuses. It's nobody else's fault. If you want the life that God has for you, go get it. If you want the pep back in your step, accept God's promise today. He will turn your mourning to dancing. He will replace your spirit of heaviness with a garment of praise. He will give you his beauty for your ashes. You must believe that.

For it is written, "Therefore if any man be in Christ, he is a new creature: old things are passed away; behold all things are become new" (2 Corinthians 5:17). This scripture means exactly what is says. *All* things are become new. This includes your past failures. There is no record of wrong for those who are in Christ. Confess yours sins and move on.

If we confess our sins, he is faithful and just to forgive us our sins, and to cleanse us from all unrighteousness.
(1 John 1:9)

Too often, we punish ourselves for past mistakes, as if we could somehow make up the wrong that we've done. We walk through each day feeling inferior. Often, years have passed but we still allow those ungodly feelings to gnaw away at our peace and joy. Reminding yourself of your past failures and choices is of no benefit to you. If you've come to Jesus and repented, you are to accept the truth about what Jesus has done for you. If you are still feeling ashamed and guilty over your past, you are not seeing yourself as God sees you. By carrying on with this behavior, you are basically denying the work of Jesus dying on the cross. You have to see yourself separated from your sins. This is the way that God sees you. This is what helped me to get over my past mistakes. I had to realize that God loves me so much—so much that he was willing to forgive me and had forgiven me a long time ago. It was me who chose to keep reminding myself of something Jehovah God had no record of. It was the enemy's way of preventing me from getting God's best for my life.

Regardless of your past or who hurt you, you have to let it go so that you can truly experience the liberty of salvation. You can be delivered from anything and everything. But until you forgive yourself and others, you won't experience the breakthrough that you need to be totally set free. God has a purpose and plan for your life. Stop allowing the enemy to blind you to God's promises because you can't seem to get the gear out of reverse. God knows everything, even the secret things of the heart that you chose not to share with anyone else. It is OK. Allow his will to be done.

For I know the thoughts that I think toward you, saith the Lord, thoughts of peace, and not of evil, to give you an expected end.

(Jeremiah 29:11)

You have an expected end. Make a decision today to press toward the mark for the prize of the high calling of God in Christ Jesus (Philippians 3:14). Stop waddling around in self-defeat. Stop pondering what you think could have or should have been. Remember, the race is not given to the swift; the battle is not to the strong (Ecclesiastes 9:11). Forget what lies behind and strain forward to what lies ahead (Philippians 3:13). Let me put it this way: if you have a pulse, you still have an opportunity for greatness. All it takes is a made-up mind. It's like the caterpillar making his journey to just the right position; know that change must come now. God has called you to something great. Forgive yourself so that you can truly walk in that calling. You will see the blessings of God overtake you.

Let us pray:

Most gracious and heavenly father, we thank you for your wondrous works and your mighty acts. We are most grateful that you stand ready and willing to forgive us of our past imperfections. Now we ask for the grace to truly forgive ourselves. Empower us to be overcomers. You said in your word that the former things have passed away and all things have been made new. Thank you, Lord Jesus, for making us brand-new. In Jesus's mighty name, we have prayed. Amen.

CHAPTER THREE

Live on Purpose

*Efforts and courage are not enough
without purpose and direction.*
—John F. Kennedy[1]

Now that we have discussed the importance of personal acceptance and forgiveness, it's time to evaluate our present reality. Have you come to a place in your life where you are no longer satisfied with where you are? Do you feel as if there is something else out there somewhere waiting for you, but you have no idea what it is or how to get there? Are you seeking God for purpose and direction? You may have realized by now that there is something peculiar about you. You know that God has called you out to do something for his kingdom, yet you are not sure what. Friend, this is your appointed time to discover what you are carrying. There is something inside of you that causes the enemy of your soul to tremble at the thought of you discovering it. The good news is that God stands ready and willing to reveal it to you. But it will require your attention and trust. I can bet you that whatever it is, is standing right in front of you, simply waiting for you to recognize it. God wants you to dream big and accomplish big things for his kingdom. If you are ready to surrender everything in order to receive the life that God has for you, even your wildest dreams will be within reach. God has promised to withhold no good thing from those who walk uprightly.

For the Lord God is a sun and shield; the Lord will give grace and glory; no good thing will He withhold from them that walk uprightly.

(Psalm 84:11)

God has uniquely tasked you for his kingdom. Now what will you do with what he has given you? Will you spend the rest of your days wandering around aimlessly? Will you go to your grave filled with dreams and visions that never came to pass? Will you keep what God placed inside of you all to yourself or are you ready to change the world? I pray that you are ready to change the world. God uses ordinary people like you and me to do extraordinary works every day.

Remember, you must someday give an account of what God has entrusted you with. Will you be as the steward who had one talent and went and buried it in the ground or will you be as the steward who was given five talents and doubled them to ten? Let's take a look at it in the book of Matthew.

For the kingdom of heaven is as a man travelling into a far country, who called his own servants, and delivered unto them his goods. And unto one he gave five talents, to another two, and to another one; to every man according to his several ability; and straightway took his journey. Then he that had received the five talents went and traded with the same, and made them other five talents. And likewise he that had received two, he also gained other two. But he that had received one went and digged in the earth, and hid his lord's money. After a long time the lord of those servants cometh, and reckoneth with them. And so he that had received five talents came and brought other five talents, saying, Lord, thou deliveredst unto me five talents: behold, I have gained beside them five talents more. His lord said unto him, well done, thou good and faithful servant: thou hast been faithful over a few things, I will make thee ruler over many things: enter thou into the joy of thy lord. He also that had received two talents came and said, Lord, thou deliveredst unto me two talents: behold, I have gained two other talents beside them. His lord said unto him, well done, good and faithful servant; thou hast been faithful over a few things, I will make thee ruler over many things: enter thou into the joy of thy lord. Then he which had received the one talent came and said, Lord, I knew thee that thou art an hard man, reaping where thou hast not sown, and gathering where thou hast not strawed: And I was afraid, and went and hid thy talent in the earth: lo, there thou hast that is thine. His lord answered and said unto him, Thou wicked and slothful servant, thou knewest that I reap where I sowed not, and gather where I have not strawed: Thou oughtest therefore to have put my money to the exchangers, and then at my coming I should have received mine own with usury. Take therefore the talent from him, and give it unto him which hath ten talents. For unto every one that hath shall be given, and he shall have abundance: but from him that hath not shall be taken away even that which he hath. And cast ye the unprofitable servant into outer darkness: there shall be weeping and gnashing of teeth.

(Matthew 25:14–30)

This parable confirms that in life, we're all given a different starting position. But that is of little to no significance. God knows where you started. He placed you there in the first place. You don't have to remind your creator of what you have or don't have. He knows the very number of hairs on your head. He knows your strengths and what you consider to be weaknesses. So excuses won't fly with God. What we are given is not what is important. What matters is what we do with what God has entrusted us with. The master in the parable praised the first two for being faithful. It wasn't even about the results. He said nothing about their financial wisdom. He scolded the third servant for being slothful. Listen up: being lazy will not get God's work done. You've got to be a go-getter. There are no ifs, ands, or buts about it. God has already placed the burning desire in your heart; will you go after it relentlessly? Stop the excuses. You must learn to make things work with what you have right now, not with what you hope to have five years from now. There will never be a perfect time. It will never feel just right. It's not supposed to. This is why you must trust the spirit of God living inside of you. He will never lead you astray. He loves you way too much to leave you out there, confused and lost, while you're desperately trying to seek out his will for your life. That's not the way God handles business.

You were chosen by God for a specific reason. It's up to you to seek out that reason. But I must forewarn you: this task is not for wimps. It's not for the people who want to just sit back and see what happens with their lives. The task of fulfilling your destiny is for the resilient. It's designed for those who will not accept *no* for an answer. It's for those who are willing to march around the wall of Jericho until it crumbles down. It's for those who see a closed door and decide to kick it down. You've got to want it bad enough to feel like Jacob. "God, I won't let go until you bless me." You have to make a decision to persist no matter the obstacle. You must not lose sight of that thing that will bring you peace, joy, and fulfillment. It's not about spending your life being what your great-grandmother wanted you to be. It's not about the life that your parents may have planned for you. This is about living the life that God designed uniquely for you. The journey will be well worth it.

Let us pray:

Most gracious and heavenly father, we come before you now as humble as we know how. Lord, we welcome the Holy Spirit in to guide us as we travel the dark road of self-discovery and personal development. Father God, it is our desire to do the very thing that you placed us here on earth to do. Give us the ability to endure. Grant us the grace to get the job done no matter the obstacles that we must overcome. In Jesus's name, we have prayed. Amen.

CHAPTER FOUR

Alabaster Box

Inside every human being there
are treasures to unlock.
—Mike Huckabee[1]

And being in Bethany in the house of
Simon the leper, as he sat at meat, there
came a woman having an alabaster box
of ointment of spikenard very precious;
and she brake the box, and poured it
on his head. And there were some that
had indignation within themselves, and
said, why was this waste of the ointment
made? For it might have been sold for
more than three hundred pence, and
have been given to the poor. And they
murmured against her. And Jesus said,
Let her alone; why trouble ye her? She
hath wrought a good work on me. For
ye have the poor with you always, and

whensoever ye will ye may do them
good: but me ye have not always.

(Mark 14:3–7)

Mary gave her best, most costly possession to Jesus.
Mary could've simply taken the lid off of the alabaster
box so that it could've later been used for something
else, but instead she made a complete sacrifice and
broke the box. Judas and the other disciples criticized
Mary for her actions. But to Mary, it mattered not. She
expressed no regret, even when it was pointed out that
the precious oils could have been sold to help the poor.
After pouring out the oil, she stooped down to anoint
Jesus's feet, loosening the tresses of her hair. This
was an indication of unusual selflessness. So why did
Mary do it? Why was she willing to give up her most
costly possession to Jesus although she was already a
believer? She didn't have to lavish him with fine oils
to prove her love. But she did. She chose to release
her earthly treasure in order to truly bless the Lord.
Aren't you ready to bless the Lord? Take a moment and
think about what's most precious to you. What's inside
of your alabaster box? Are you willing to release it?
Are you willing to step out of your comfort zone and
do what you have been chosen and purposed to do? I
pray that your answer is yes. Just as Mary experienced
criticism for her act of selflessness, we must expect
the same. Many will simply not understand. If it was
meant for them to understand, God would've called
them instead of you. So stop seeking the support of

others. You must lean and depend on the one who is in constant communication with God: the Holy Spirit. The Holy Spirit gives you power and direction. You cannot rely on your own wisdom to figure it out.

Let me share a brief story with you.

A while back, one of my closest friends seemed to catch hell from every side. The worst of the worst always seemed to find her. She was nearing the completion of her nursing studies but still couldn't catch a break. It was one thing and then the next. She phoned me one evening, devastated. She'd just gotten word that she would no longer be eligible for financial aid. Tearfully, she exclaimed, "How will I ever pay for school?" I listened empathetically and then told her to relax and allow God to be in control. She'd come too close to give up now. Greatness was in her and could only be held down temporarily. She thanked me for always providing an encouraging word. A few days went by. She then phoned back. Someone in the financial aid office from her school informed her that she may be eligible for a full paid scholarship. Let me interject by stating that God always has a ram in the bush. We just have to trust what we cannot trace.

One of the scholarship requirements was for her to submit a personal statement explaining her financial hardship and why she should be considered for the award. She immediately asked me to assist her with writing the letter. Of course I agreed. I'd actually been writing letters of all kinds for people for years. So I knew that my writing abilities were pretty good. At this same time, I'd been praying for God to show me the thing that I was supposed to be doing here on earth. I knew that I had been called to be more than a nurse. I just had an inner feeling that there was so much more that I had to offer to the world. Yet I really couldn't put my finger on it. My friend gave me the personal statement form, and I placed it on my computer desk, where it sat for months. I was finishing my doctoral degree at the time and could not make it a priority. I knew that before the deadline, we would get it done. I remember telling her to just jot down some ideas and then I would help her format it. So she tried but just couldn't get it going.

Finally one day, she stopped by my home, and while she was there, I felt the Holy Spirit nudge me to write the letter. I opened my laptop, and before I knew it, I'd written about fifteen hundred words about my friend's life. It was as if I had become her. As I read it back to her, tears filled her eyes. She said, "I'm crying about my own story; it's so beautifully written." I knew that whoever read her statement would come to know Jesus in a more intimate way. Throughout the statement, I continuously showed reverence to the Lord and acknowledged his grace and mercy. I wasn't sure what the organization was expecting from the applicants. All I knew is that I had to follow the lead of the spirit of God living on the inside of me. When I finished, we thanked God, and I gave the statement to her for submission.

Months passed by, and finally one day I looked down at my phone and received a text from her exclaiming that she had been awarded a full scholarship. I was thrilled! I called her, and she explained all of the details. She told me that she received a phone call from the organization telling her of the good news. She said the lady on the other end was in tears. She said that everyone who read her story had the same reaction. She also informed my friend that she was one of eighty applicants selected from a pool of eight hundred throughout the nation. The lady told her that the selection process was very tedious and had about eight phases, each with a different panel of readers. I was so thankful to God for the favor that was shown to her.

I then asked her to read the letter to me. It had been months, and I honestly had forgotten what was written. As she read it, my eyes began to swell with tears. By the time she finished, I couldn't even speak. I remember looking up toward heaven and thanking God. The story touched my heart. It was as if I'd never heard it before. I told her that my prayer had been answered. I felt a sense of knowing in my spirit. I knew then what God had chosen me to do. For whatever reason, God gifted me with the ability to touch the hearts of others through the art of effective communication. All along, these precious oils had been hidden inside of me.

You see, the enemy will plant seeds of doubt in your mind. He will attempt to downplay your task. He will try his best to get you to believe that your gift is no big deal. Remember, I had been writing for years. I had been encouraging people for years. I was always the go-to person. Even at times when I was in the midst of my own crisis somehow I could overlook my pain and say just the right thing to give someone else hope. It was a gift!

I ended that phone conversation knowing what my purpose was in life. God was calling me higher. I had so many unanswered questions yet I surrendered. I stopped trying to figure it out. The same goes for you. Please stop trying to figure it out. It won't make sense right now. But know this: if God calls you to do it, the provisions are already made. I had no earthly idea that the very same letter that I wrote would turn around and set me free. You too will have an *aha* moment. You will come to a place where everything begins to make sense. You will understand why you are so passionate about certain things. You will begin to recognize that some of the things that others struggle with will come easily to you. Just take some time and think about it. Personal reflection is very important. Light a candle, sit back, and spend some time with the Lord. He will share his secrets with you.

The secret of the LORD is with them that fear him; and he will shew them his covenant.

(Psalm 25:14)

Here's the important thing to remember: any time we want to hear from God, the method is the same—praying, reading the Bible, and meditating on his word. Be a good listener. God will not leave you to wander around, lost in the wilderness, if you truly seek him with your whole heart.

Be mindful that the greatest people ever heard of did not wake up one morning to discover that they were great. They may have known that there was something unique about them, but it still didn't happen overnight. It's a painstaking process. God doesn't just throw things in your lap. He gives you the gift, but it's up to you to cultivate and grow it. This is why you must know what you are carrying.

I remember listening to a sermon by T. D. Jakes one morning. In it, he talked about how even as a young boy, he would preach to the soap dish and washrag in his bathroom. Preaching was in him. Did he start out preaching to the masses? No. Was his first church a mega church? No. He had to go through his process, just as we each have to go through ours. The greatness hidden inside of his alabaster box was not revealed to the world until many years later.

Friend, God placed precious oils inside each of us for his glory. We must do as Mary did and break the box, not simply remove the lid and replace it as convenient. All God wants is for us to lend our ears to his divine instruction. God will bless your socks off in exchange for your act of submission.

Let us pray:

God, allow us to discover what precious oils we are carrying inside of our spiritual alabaster boxes. Just as Mary poured the oil onto the head of Jesus, allow us to pour our oils onto your people so that we can add value and honor to their lives. We ask that the Holy Spirit will guide us into our divine purpose as we constantly seek your wisdom. Nothing, God, is more precious than living a life that is pleasing unto you. In Jesus's name, we have prayed. Amen.

CHAPTER FIVE

The Vision

The eyes of your understanding being
enlightened; that ye may know what is the
hope of his calling, and what the riches of
the glory of his inheritance in the saints
—Ephesians 1:18

Do you realize that you can have 20/20 vision in the
natural world and still be spiritually blind? In the book
of Ephesians, Paul emphasizes how critical it is for the
eyes of your heart to be open. If the eyes of your heart
are not open, you will remain clueless to what God has
called you to be. The scripture says, "That ye may know
the hope of his calling" (Eph 1:18). Therefore, it is safe
to say that when God created you, he had a hope of what
you would become. In order to know what that hope is,
you must be able to see what God sees concerning you.
The tricky part here is that we often think our spiritual
vision is on point when, in actuality, it is not. Remember
the blind man from Bethsaida?

And he cometh to Bethsaida; and
they bring a blind man unto him, and
besought him to touch him. And he took
the blind man by the hand, and led him
out of the town; and when he had spit on
his eyes, and put his hands upon him,
he asked him if he saw ought. And he
looked up, and said, I see men as trees,
walking. After that he put his hands
again upon his eyes, and made him look
up: and he was restored, and saw every
man clearly. And he sent him away to
his house, saying, neither go into the
town, nor tell it to any in the town

(Mark 8:22–26)

When Jesus laid hands on the blind man the first
time and asked what he saw, the man responded, "I
see men as trees walking." Then Jesus put his hands
on him again, and this time he saw things clearly. We
know that Jesus is the ultimate healer. In the Bible, he
healed more blindness than any other illness. So why
do you think there is record of this partial healing? Do
you think that possibly God is using this story to teach
us something? Would it be safe to say that sometimes
we may think that we can see things clearly when this
is not so? When the man said what he saw the first time,
he probably thought that his vision was clear. Yet by his
confession, Jesus knew that he needed another touch.
Sometimes it takes another touch from the Lord. In

order to receive that second touch, we have to be honest with ourselves about where we are, just as the blind man from Bethsaida was. He admitted that he could see, yet he obviously was not seeing clearly. After Jesus put his hands upon him again, he was completely restored and saw everything clearly. After he received his total healing, he was instructed not to go back to Bethsaida.

You too will come to a place in your life when you can no longer go back to your old way of doing things. Your circle of friends will become few. Your loved ones won't understand you. You will know in your spirit that you have heard from the Lord and sensed in your heart what you have been called to do. You will realize that your spiritual vision has been corrected because you no longer see things the way that you used to. You will know that God is doing a great work in you. Ultimately it is your responsibility to ensure that whatever it is that you have been called to do comes to pass. In other words, you have to make something happen. It will not come easy.

The kingdom of heaven suffers violence and the violent take it by force.

(Matthew 11:12)

Where do you see yourself going? Did you know that nothing happens until it happens in someone's mind first? This is another reason why it is so critical to have a shared vision with God. What's your plan? Whatever it is that you believe God has called you to do, you must take it by force. You have to write your vision down and make it plain (Habakkuk 2:2). Once you've written it down, you have to work for it. Bottled up thoughts in your head will not take you there. You can't just lollygag around and expect something to happen. The enemy of your existence is not going to just passively sit back and allow you to walk into your harvest. He's not going to cheer you on and encourage you to realize that you have been chosen by God. As a matter of fact, he's going to do everything within his power to stop you. He doesn't fight fair, either. He will hit you below the waistline any chance that he gets. This is why you must watch as well as pray (Mark 13:33). You must put on the full armor of God that you may be able to stand against the schemes of the devil (Ephesians 6:11).

Get moving. I can't stress it enough. You can't just continue saying, "One day, I'm going to do this," or "Someday, I'm going to that." It doesn't work that way. Before you know it, days, weeks, and years go by, and you have done nothing. I can assure you that the needed resources will not just fall from the sky when the timing is right. Whatever it is that you see yourself doing, you have to invest in it right now. Not tomorrow, not next week—right now. If you can see yourself doing it, you can do it. You have to start somewhere. Having a general idea of how you would like your life to go will not get you there. You have to make the necessary strides to see your vision through. If you don't feed it, it will die (Proverbs 29:18).

What are you doing every day to make sure that your vision comes to pass? Is it even a priority for you? If it's not a priority for you, what makes you think that it will be a priority for God? Yes, we need God to bring our visions to pass, but there is a difference between waiting on the manifestation and being lazy. You cannot expect your vision to be fulfilled without any effort, work, or obedience on your part. Faith without works is dead (James 2:26).

Remember what happened in the book of Genesis when the people began to build the Tower of Babel? Let's take a look:

> And they said, Go to, let us build us a city and a tower, whose top [may reach] unto heaven; and let us make us a name, lest we be scattered abroad upon the face of the whole earth. And the LORD came down to see the city and the tower, which the children of men builded. And the LORD said, Behold, the people [is] one, and they have all one language; and this they begin to do: and now nothing will be restrained from them, which they have imagined to do.
>
> (Genesis 11:4–6)

This is a perfect example of what happens when people share one vision. They would have been successful in building a tower to heaven had God not intervened. The scripture states, "And now nothing will be restrained from them, which they have imagined to do." So you see, this again confirms that everything starts in the mind. They first imagined building it, and then they began to build it. How much more powerful would it be to share God's vision for you? Then, nothing shall be impossible for you.

Often, distractions come up and things happen in our lives that cause us to lose sight of our vision. We can sometimes become so consumed with the hustle and bustle of everyday life that we stop thinking about our visions. We may have started out with good intentions, but somewhere along the way, for one reason or another, we lost sight. It doesn't matter how off-the-wall it may sound to someone else; if you have a vision, you must go after it. If you hold it in your heart long enough, you will hold it in your hand. Close your eyes and visualize already having it. By doing this, the law of attraction will begin the creative process of forming that thought into a reality. Your subconscious mind will become more aware of opportunities that will bring you the things you think about.

Let me share a story with you that truly helped me to realize the importance of having a vision and being sure to see that vision through. Ever heard of the pharmacist Dr. John Pemberton? Maybe … maybe not, right? Well perhaps I should ask an easier question. Ever heard of Coca-Cola Classic? I'm sure just about everyone is familiar with the refreshing, invigorating taste of a good old Coke. Well, in 1886, Dr. John Pemberton invented the soft drink in a three-legged brass pot in his very own backyard. The soft drink was first sold to the public at the soda fountain in a local Atlanta pharmacy that same year. It is estimated that a mere nine servings of the drink were sold daily. The first year of sales for the now world-renowned soft drink totaled a whopping fifty bucks. Unfortunately, it cost Dr. Pemberton more than seventy dollars in expenses. So, we can just say that the first year of sales was a loss. Now how about that? The Coca-Cola Company, which is now all over the world, did nothing the first year of its existence.[1]

As time went on, Dr. Pemberton became more interested in expanding the market for French Wine Coca, a product based on the formula for another extremely popular coca-based beverage, than for his own invention. Although Pemberton may have envisioned a future for his soft drink, he soon began selling his interest in the formula. In 1887, another Atlanta pharmacist and businessman, Asa Candler, bought the formula for Coca-Cola for a mere twenty-three hundred dollars. By the late 1890s, Coca-Cola was one of America's most popular fountain drinks, largely due to Candler's aggressive marketing of the product. With Mr. Candler in charge, the Coca-Cola Company increased syrup sales by over 4000 percent between 1890 and 1900. Candler was a firm believer in advertising. He used the same marketing principle as Pemberton but expanded on it by distributing thousands of coupons for a complimentary glass of Coca-Cola. He promoted the product relentlessly, distributing souvenir fans, calendars, clocks, urns, and countless novelties, all portraying the trademark.

The business continued to grow, and in 1894, the first syrup manufacturing plant outside Atlanta was opened in Dallas, Texas. Others were later opened in Chicago and Los Angeles the following year. Needless to say, the demand for Coca-Cola continued to increase. In the year 1919, Candler sold Coke for 25 million dollars. Not a bad investment, right? Today, Coca-Cola produces more than two hundred brands in more than four hundred countries. So what was the difference between the two men? It was the same product. The same opportunities were available to both. You could even say that Pemberton was more talented in that he actually invented the product. So why did one man fail and the other succeed? Pemberton failed because he lost sight. Sadly, he never completely grasped the potential of the beverage he created. He died just two years after his invention. Another man was able to catch the vision and run with it. Will you catch your own vision and run with it? Or will you allow someone else to do so? Will you continue to procrastinate until you see the invention that you thought of in your mind ten years ago created by someone else who is now receiving the Nobel Prize for it? I would hope not.

I remember when I first embraced the idea of writing books. As I began to tell people about my vision, I was laughed at. I would then hear the infamous, "Well, let me know how it all goes." That meant "don't quit your day job." What I realized after experiencing that same talk with countless people is that you can't share your vision with everybody. Some people will just have to find out after the fact. I then began to ask myself what I was doing to carry out my vision. Heck, I wasn't even writing. I just kept saying, "One day, one day, one day." Finally, I cried out to the Lord and promised that no matter what, "I am going to write every day as if my life depends on it, because I realize that it does." Please do not expect to just suddenly arrive at *one day*. That location cannot be programmed into even the most advanced GPS system.

Let me share this. I was sitting around the kitchen table one evening with some guests. It just so happened that all of the guys had gone outside and gathered around the grill. So it was just us ladies. I began to talk about how faithful the Lord is in answering prayer. I went on to talk about how important it is to dream big. Not only are you supposed to dream big, but you are supposed to act on those dreams. You have to believe that you can do what lies within your heart. Immediately, all of the ladies began to share what they would really like to do with their lives. Some wanted to own their own businesses, others wanted to become authors, and so forth. I then posed the question, "What's stopping you? What is it that's standing in your way of coming alive? What's the worst thing that could happen if you stepped out of your comfort zone and began to do the thing that has been in your heart?" For me, I was afraid of failure and rejection. I felt that even if I gathered up the nerve to finally begin to write books, would I be good enough? Would I ever find a publisher? What would I write about? Did I even know the Bible well enough to try to become a Christian author? If I dared to stand on platforms and deliver empowerment speeches would the audience be receptive? I made up every excuse in the world to keep myself from doing what I knew God had called me to do. You see, we spend so much time trying to figure everything out. We want to already know the end from the beginning. But that's not the way it works. God reveals things to us as appropriate, not all at once.

Now ask yourself, "What is it that's hindering me?" Is it the fear of making a mistake? We learn from them, remember? It's okay to fall, but it's not okay to stay there. We have to get back up—repeatedly, if necessary. Don't allow your fears or excuses to hold you in a place of mediocrity. God is with you. You must know that if you just take a plunge out into the deep, the Lord Jesus will catch you. It is not God's desire for us to wander around feeling worthless and unfilled. It was never God's intent for us to depart this world full of hopes, dreams, and visions that were never acted upon. Just as Jesus raised Lazarus from the dead many years ago, we can experience a spiritual resurrection right now. Know that it is well with you. You are not dreaming just to be dreaming. If you have somehow stopped dreaming, please begin to dream again. It is God who placed the desire in your heart in the first place. You must believe that it will come to pass. Remember, you are God's elect. You are preferred. Your endeavors have priority.

Let us pray:

Father God, spiritually resurrect us now. Give us the grace to come forth and live a life that is prosperous and of benefit to your kingdom. Correct our spiritual vision. Allow us to see what you see. Allow us to dream again and may the Holy Spirit provide us with the strategy to fulfill those dreams. In Jesus's name. Amen.

CHAPTER SIX

Dealing with Rejection

I am thankful for all of those who said no to me. It's because of them I'm doing it myself.
—Albert Einstein[1]

Did you know that the infamous Winston Churchill failed the sixth grade and lost every single election for public office? Yet at the age of sixty-two, he became prime minister of Britain. What about Thomas Edison? He was told by his teachers that he was too stupid to ever learn anything. You see? You certainly can't listen to other people's opinions. Colonel Sanders was rejected one thousand times before establishing KFC. No one would sell his chicken. Isn't that something? Marilyn Monroe's first contract with Columbia Pictures expired because they told her she wasn't pretty or talented enough to be an actress. Did she give up? No, she did not. She later became one of the most iconic actresses of all time and is considered one of the prettiest women who ever lived. Albert Einstein didn't speak until four years of age. He could not read until he was seven years old. He was labeled *slow* and *mentally handicapped.* Yet he developed the world's most famous equation. Did you know that Dr. Seuss's first book was rejected by twenty-seven different publishers? To date, he is the most popular children's book author who ever lived. What is the common denominator amongst these people? They kept trying. They did not give up because things didn't go right the first time or maybe even the one-thousandth time. [2]

So if we know that we can succeed after being rejected, why does it still hurt so badly when someone rejects us? Why do we often feel as if the world has ended because a door closes in our faces? Do we actually believe there is not an open one nearby, awaiting our recognition? Can we not see the forest for the trees? Why do we spend years harboring unforgiveness in our hearts because we were not accepted by someone? Do we actually need their acceptance? Why do we give rejection that much power? We allow it to damage our self-esteem, and if we're not careful, we may allow it to destroy our purpose in life. When we free ourselves from the misconceptions of need driven by external forces, we free ourselves from the pain associated with rejection. Rejection in itself does not cause pain; we cause the pain by taking things personally. For this very reason, rejection is a common tool that Satan uses to destroy us. Rejection can destroy our hopes and dreams, and if we're not careful, it can *literally* destroy us.

Many people experience rejection and never recover. For some ungodly reason, we often feel the need to be accepted and validated by others. We must understand that it is not God's desire for us to ever feel rejected or abandoned. God's desire is for us to know who we really are. It's not until you know who you really are that you can begin to do the work that God has called you to do. If the enemy can keep us blinded from our purpose, his tactic was a success. I don't think that I can ever say this enough: the devil is a liar. If we want to be all that God has created us to be, then overcoming rejection and its effects is vital and absolutely essential.

Regardless of what the enemy wants us to believe, every person who has been called by God to do something great first entered a dark season of their lives. It's darkest just before dawn, right? The grimmest times of your life are actually the times when you are closest to your breakthrough. During these painful times, you are actually right on the edge of something great. When everything in you is telling you to give up; this is actually an indicator of your need to persist and believe God. You will later panic at the thought of what you almost gave up on simply because of the way things looked at the time. Remember, you cannot depend on your natural senses to guide you. We are to trust in the Lord with all of our heart and lean not on our own understanding (Proverbs 3:5).

Have you ever heard of John Kennedy Toole?

John Kennedy Toole was an American novelist from New Orleans, Louisiana, best known for his novel *A Confederacy of Dunces*. As a young, struggling author, the hopeful Toole sent his manuscript off to a New

York publishing company called Simon & Schuster. Shockingly, it immediately got the attention of the senior editor, Robert Gottlieb. Gottlieb recognized the potential of the book but felt that it wasn't quite where it should be. So he began a string of successive requests for revisions. Toole readily complied. Eventually, Gottlieb lost total interest in the novel. "With all its wonderfulness," wrote Gottlieb, "the book does not have a reason. It isn't really about anything. And that's something no one can do anything about." Heartbroken by the rejection, Toole flew to New York in an effort to plead for his book, but to no avail. He was banned from the sanctum. Simon & Schuster had no interest in publishing *A Confederacy of Dunces*, nor did anyone else. Five years later, Toole committed suicide. Some years after his death, Toole's mother set out on a seven-year mission to get her son's work published. She believed in him. Each submission to various publishers was again rejected. But she didn't give up. She then brought the manuscript to the attention of novelist Walker Percy. She was very persistent, and it has been said that she practically stalked Percy until he read it. Percy later admitted that he had hoped that the novel would've been terrible enough to discard after reading a few pages, but he was wrong. After he finished reading the manuscript, he wrote a letter to Toole's mother exclaiming how extraordinary the work was. It was Percy who ushered the book into print. Eleven years after Toole's suicide, Toole was posthumously awarded the Pulitzer Prize for Fiction.[3]

Isn't that a sad story? What makes it worse is that it actually happened. You cannot allow rejection to deter you from your destiny. It is simply a trick of the enemy. So how do you overcome it? How do you handle the disappointment of discovering that you don't add up to the world's expectation of you? What do you do when the world tells you that you are not pretty enough, or smart enough, or tall enough? What if the very thing that you've spent hours and hours laboring over is rejected in two seconds? Someone else who had no idea of the hell you've gone through just comes along and tells you that your work is worthless or that it's not unique enough. Or perhaps they don't feel as if anyone will buy it. You're made to feel inferior because you don't have a name for yourself. Well guess what? God knows your name. If God is for you, who can be against you? Tell me, are you going to accept the world telling you who you are or will you accept what God says in his word about you? This is why you must base your identity only on what the word of God says about you. If you base your identity on someone or something, you make yourself vulnerable to the damaging effects of being rejected. When we base our identity upon what the word of God has to say about us, we are no longer subject to rejection. We develop immunity. God will never reject you. No matter the circumstance, you are precious in the eyes of God.

As you come to him, a living stone rejected by men but in the sight of God chosen and precious.

(1 Peter 2:4 ESV)

Even if your mother or father rejected you, know that you have a heavenly father who will never, ever turn his back on you. The Lord will always take you in.

For my father and my mother have forsaken me, but the Lord will take me in.

(Psalm 27:10 ESV)

Tell me, do you fear rejection more than you desire success? After a few rejections—or for some people, after only one rejection—we automatically assume our objective is more difficult than it actually is. If we perceive that something is really difficult, we have a tendency to give up on it completely. Remember, you may be told *no* a thousand times, but there is always a *yes* somewhere. Do you desire to answer the call of God badly enough to find the *yes*? One acceptance can put you back on the road to success. Remember, even what seems difficult is not. If God appointed you to do a great work for his kingdom, know that the provision has already been made. There is a ram in the bush. Look for it. Take a moment and thank God for his faithfulness. He will do just as he promised you.

Let us pray:

Father God, we will no longer be deterred by failure. We realize that with you, absolutely nothing is impossible. We decree and declare that no devil in hell is going to stop what you have purposed us to do. In Jesus's name, we have prayed. Amen.

CHAPTER SEVEN

Do What You Love

Let a man have what he will, and do what he will, it signifies nothing without charity; which surely implies that charity is the great thing, and that everything which has not charity in some way contained or implied in it is nothing.
—Jonathan Edwards[1]

For many years, I had no idea what I was carrying. I knew that I had been called to do something but was clueless about what it was. Remember, I was too busy coveting my sister's gift to seek God about my own. So how do you know? What is the thing that you would enjoy doing even if there was no money involved? What makes you tick? What gives you a sense of fulfillment? What is it that you love? That's most likely the thing that you have been called to do.

There is no clear-cut plan for figuring out what you love doing. However, you'll know what it is when you find it. Once I realized that my true passion was to encourage and motivate the people of God, it made sense why I went from loving work to hating the idea of having to report there every morning. I was grateful for my job but felt as if I was not maximizing my potential. I felt smothered. I no longer fit in. When you find yourself in a similar predicament, it is time to seek the guidance of the Holy Spirit as to what's next. It's OK to feel uncertain as long as you know that God is leading you. It's OK to be laughed at. Others are supposed to think that you're crazy. Remember, it's your calling, not theirs. So don't expect others to understand. Even those closest to you may not support you, but it's OK. It all comes down to one question: how bad do you want it? Do you want it so bad that you are willing to become relentless about it?

I was talking to a friend one afternoon about this very topic. She is gifted in the area of fashion. She has the unique ability to put colors and trends together in a way that baffles me. She knows that she has the gift. She's been this way since she was a little kid. So I asked her what it is about fashion that makes her buzz. She said, "When I go out to a store or shopping mall, I just get a high off of putting unique things together, even if it's not for me. I just love it!"

I then began to give her some ideas of how to put her gift to work. I thought about it all night and into the next day. I remember telling her, "Encouraging you is what makes me high." It's like I get a buzz off of empowering others. It's difficult to explain, and everyone's passion is different. The feeling that you get when you're doing the thing that you truly desire is priceless. It's beyond words. You just know that you're finally doing the thing that you love. Don't let anybody relegate you to a corner and tell you what you can or can't do. Who are they? Can they walk on water? No, they cannot.

Living in such a fast-paced world makes us expect things to happen overnight. Wouldn't it be great to just jump out there today and say, "You know what, this is it. Everything that I've desired will happen today, right now." Well, yes, that would be nice, but that's not typically the way our heavenly father operates. We have to first mature to the point where we can handle what God truly has for us. There are some things that you pray about, and God moves immediately. Then there are other things that God will not do until you have truly convinced him that you are serious. God honors persistence. Do you wake up every morning with the same prayer on your lips about the thing that drives you? While you're driving in your car, are you reminding God about it? Are you thanking him for the success of whatever it is? During the day, do you get off to yourself and pray about it some more. Are you putting actions with your prayers? Are you telling God, "Lord, I have no idea how this is going to come to pass, but I know that I won't give up until it does"? Stop looking at your own limitations. None of that matters. If there is any way to turn a situation around, prayer will do it. Jesus said, "Whatsoever you desire when you pray, believe that you have received it and you will have it" (Mark 11:24). If you pray according to that desire, you shall have it. There is power in your passion. This is why the enemy tries to discourage you. It's your passion that moves God. If the enemy can rob you of your passion, he can rob you of your destiny. Don't let him. Fight in the spirit for what you know is rightfully yours. The devil is full of fluff. He's already defeated. You know that.

What are you willing to sacrifice? Are you willing to lay it all on the line for what you know God has placed in your heart? How persistent are you? There are no rest periods. You've got to drive that thing until you see it come to pass.

Let's look at the parable of the persistent widow:

> And he spake a parable unto them to this end, that men ought always to pray, and not to faint Saying, There was in a city a judge, which feared not God, neither regarded man:
>
> And there was a widow in that city; and she came unto him, saying, Avenge me of mine adversary. And he would not for a while: but afterward he said within himself, Though I fear not God, nor regard man; Yet because this widow troubleth me, I will avenge her, lest by her continual coming she weary me.
>
> (Luke 18:1–5)

In this parable, the widow utters five words, "Avenge me of my adversary," to a judge who has no fear of God. If he had no fear of God, then I would think that it's pretty safe to say he had no relationship with God. Yet eventually he honored her request. Why? Well it says that she continuously *troubled* him. In other words, she came to him over and over until, quite frankly, she got on his nerves and he gave up. He realized he had to give her what she was asking for if he ever wanted to have another day of peace in his lifetime. So what's the moral of the story? You have to decide what you want and then you have to continuously speak it into the atmosphere as well as pray to God concerning it. This is not a time to do sprints; it's a time to prepare for a spiritual marathon. You must be willing to endure. You have to be willing to pray about it until something happens. If you see no change, keep praying. Most important, don't give up.

Let me share a story with you. I once heard about a lady who developed a passion for flying at a very early age. She often watched small planes roll down the runway and then up and away into the heavens from a small-town airport near her childhood home. She longed to know the feeling of not being held down by anything, even gravity. She often dreamed of becoming a pilot but felt that it was only for rich people and certainly not for women. She was also told that she had to have perfect vision. So in her mind, she had three strikes against her. She was not rich, she was not a male, and she wore glasses. Let me pause for a moment; please recognize that these are all self-defeating thoughts. This is one of the typical strategies used by Satan to dissuade us from going after our dreams. If he can convince us that we are disqualified from the beginning, we will never truly pursue what God has for us. Now back to the story. Feeling disqualified, the lady lost sight of her dreams. She accepted that she would never fly, and as a result, she felt as if her life had no purpose. But the desire simply would not go away. The more she tried to shake it, the more intense it became. So she began to seek God about it. For the longest time, it seemed as if nothing changed. Was God listening? Then one day, the lady was at a local fair and noticed a line of people snaking across a field. She discovered that a school was selling plane rides as a fundraiser. The cost was very inexpensive. So she bought a ticket. When her turn came, she was escorted into the front passenger seat of a nice little four-seater airplane. As she settled in, she glanced at the pilot. Low and behold, he was wearing eyeglasses! She talked with the pilot as they taxied across the field. She told the pilot that she'd always wanted to fly but didn't think that she could because she wore glasses. The pilot assured her that it would not be a problem. He told her that learning to fly was fun but required a lot of work, time, and money.

When the lady returned home that evening, she couldn't forget the words that the pilot had spoken. She'd always wanted to fly but had never actually looked into it. She asked herself, "What's stopping me?" She then realized that it could only be one thing: herself. She didn't believe in herself. She checked out books about flying from the local library and learned the requirements for a pilot's license. She memorized the functioning of all of the gauges and controls on an airplane. She also read about other female aviators. Amelia Earhart had been her idol growing up. The only thing holding her back now was a lack of money. Flying lessons were expensive.

One day as she was driving through the countryside not far from where she lived, she noticed a small airport that she'd never seen before. She then saw a little sign that read "Introducing flying lessons for $50." She couldn't believe it. She could afford that. She jotted down the phone number, and after a few days of mustering up courage, she made the phone call. A man answered and told her that he was available the next afternoon. She told her parents about it, and they thought that she was crazy. They also told her that flying was dangerous. But the lady had made up her mind. Nothing would stop her now. She met the middle-aged man at the airport, and after a short introduction, she took the pilot's seat. Within minutes, and of course after instruction, she and the gentleman taxied down the runway. As the little plane lifted off of the ground, the lady's heart soared with it. She was flying an airplane! She said that it felt like a miracle. It took some time to get her pilot's license, but eventually she did. Through it all, she learned something more important than how to fly a plane. She learned how to believe in herself. She realized through this experience just how much God loved her.

Now let me ask you this: is there a desire in your heart to do something that simply won't go away? No matter how hard you try not to think about it, does it keep coming back? Will you go after it, no matter the odds ... no matter who tells you that you will never qualify? Will you overcome the most difficult obstacles so that you too can experience a miracle? Don't settle. If you don't build your own dreams, you will help build someone else's. You must have the faith to know that God has your back. He is with you always, no matter how it looks. You must find and do what you love.

Let us pray:

Father God, give us the grace to do what we really love. No matter the obstacles, help us to realize that you are right there with us. You promised in your word to give us the desires of our hearts if we delight ourselves in you. We thank you for that promise. In Jesus's name, we have prayed. Amen.

CHAPTER EIGHT

Take the Risks

Only those who will risk going too far can possibly find out how far one can go.
—T. S. Eliot[1]

Back in the day, I had a friend who loved to play poker and was actually pretty good at it. I would often sit back and watch the game, wishing I had the know-how to play a hand or two. Often, he had a losing hand but somehow still managed to fool other players into folding. He was so good about keeping a poker face. Others could not predict his moves. So what contributed to his success in the game? It's simple; he was a risk-taker. He didn't focus on what he could lose; he focused on what he could gain. If he lost it all, he just lost it all. But if he played his cards right, he often got up from the table smiling.

Life is a lot like a poker game. In the end, it all comes down to what you are willing to risk. However, in poker, you can always play another hand. In life, you may not always have that option. You can get in there and do something with the hand that you've been dealt or let the world go on as if you never existed and win without you. It's just that simple.

So how do you learn to play? How do you ever get from where you are to where you want to be? How do you get out of the planning stage? Why does it seem so difficult to make something happen? Well, this is exactly what the enemy wants us to believe. He wants us to believe that doing a great work for the Lord is too risky. There's too much involved. It's best to just learn to be content with where you are right now. These are the lies that he will feed you. Why? Because the devil is a vision thief. If he can convince you that what's in your heart will never manifest; then he wins. He uses the same old tricks over and over. But you know what? It's time for us to pull a fast one on him. It's time for us to declare civil war with the forces that have been working overtime to hold us back. You have to be willing to take the risks. You have to show God that no matter what; your faith is immovable. Make a decision to stand firm. In doing so, God will be well pleased with you. He will uphold you with his righteous right hand (Isaiah 41:10). God will honor the heart of one who truly tries. You have to make up your mind that no matter what, you're going all the way with this thing. Once you do, there's not a demonic force strong enough to throw you off course.

Take a moment and picture yourself at the Kentucky Derby. The horses are all lined up and ready to go. They have trained hard and are ready to cross the finish line. But wait, what's that across their eyes? Are they blindfolded? I've watched plenty of horse races and never thought much about the blinders that you often see them wearing. It never crossed my mind until one of my best friends told me one evening that she was wearing spiritual blinders. I looked at her a little funny. She went on to say, "You know, like the ones the horses wear when they are racing? I'm not looking to my left or right; I'm staying focused on what God has called me to do." I kept thinking about what she said. I kept picturing a vision that I'd seen plenty of times: horses lined up to race, but with what appeared to be little blindfolds covering their eyes. I wonder why I'd never thought to ask why this is so. Does it make sense to run a race blindfolded? How far could you run without sight? I imagine not very far. So what's the rationale?

Horses have eyes on the sides of their heads instead of in front. They have peripheral vision because they are hunted in nature. As a result, during a race, they can end up running off-course unless they are made to remain focused. It has been said that the whole idea of a horse wearing blinders originated from a preacher having a wager with a friend. The preacher bet his friend that the horse could walk up the stairs in his home. He was right; the horse walked up the stairs without a problem. But when the preacher tried to lead him back down, the horse would not budge. Next, the preacher covered the horse's head and led him down. The horse followed. The preacher then realized that by covering all or part of the horse's vision, the horse would take chances it would not normally take. So what's my point? Just like the horse, we cannot rely on what we can see with our natural eyes because if we do, we won't budge. We have to put on our spiritual blinders in order to stay focused on what God has shown us in the spirit. By doing so, we become more inclined to take risks.

Have you ever heard of Nik Wallenda? Nik is a seventh-generation high-wire artist and is part of the famous Flying Wallendas circus family. By all means, he is a risk taker. I held my breath just watching the videotaped performances of him crossing Niagara Falls and the Grand Canyon, even though I already knew the outcome. Nik's family is no stranger to death-defying feats, which in some instances have ended in great tragedy. Nik's great-grandfather, Karl Walenda, fell during a televised performance in Puerto Rico at the age of seventy-three. Nik has also lost several other family members, including a cousin and uncle during wire walking accident. Nik acknowledges his gift as one that only God can give. It's who he is. His determination to do God's will for his life overshadows any possible fear. If you ever have a chance to watch Nik perform, you will hear him audibly thank the Lord Jesus throughout his venture. It's an amazing feat that he does with such grace. It blesses my heart just to watch.[2]

God may not have called you to walk a two-inch wire fifteen hundred feet above the Grand Canyon, but he did call you to do something. Whatever it is that you have been appointed to do will require you to step out of your comfort zone. It will require preparation. It will require determination. You have to be willing to take the risks.

As I watched Nik cross the Grand Canyon on video, the wind began to pick up. His balancing pole began to tip. But he somehow steadied himself. You would immediately wonder how he is able to remain calm and focused under those conditions. Well, Nik prepares for the wind and rain by using wind machines during practice sessions; they can get up to 55 mph. He has trained through torrential downpours. What are you doing to ensure that you will be able to withstand unfavorable conditions? Will you lose focus if a storm begins to rage in your life on the way to your destiny? What happens if spiritual wind gusts begin to blow profusely? Will you let that steer you away from your God-given purpose? Expect the unexpected. But know that God will bring you through.

Let us pray:

Father God, grant us the courage to take risks. We realize that because we are hidden in Christ Jesus, we absolutely cannot lose. There is only gain. You said that he who leaves his house, or father, or mother, or wife, or children, or land for your sake and for the sake of the gospel will receive a one hundred fold return now. We thank you for all that shall be given to us as a result of us answering the calls upon our lives. We ask you for the grace to do just what you placed us here to do. We love you, Lord. In Jesus's name, we have prayed. Amen.

CHAPTER NINE

The Adversary

When you ask God for a promotion,
he will schedule an adversary.
—Mike Murdock[1]

For six months straight, day in and out, I prayed to God for a promotion at my job. It wasn't necessarily for the increase in pay, although that would've been an added bonus. The truth of the matter is, I simply wanted peace. I was functioning in a management position that had turned into a nightmare. When I first started the new position, I was so thankful to God. I had such hopes and dreams of turning the department around and getting things on track. As time went on, I began to realize that I may not be best suited for the task. It was just too much. All who know me will tell you that I am probably one of the most optimistic people that they know. So if I say the position was too much, then it really was. Being that I am not a quitter, I decided to pray to God for a way of escape instead of folding. I felt that I had given my all, yet it was not valued.

It seemed as if the more I prayed, the more hell broke loose. I began to be falsely accused of things. One guy at work made his mind up that I was the enemy. He was convinced that I'd done something to him that I actually knew nothing about. I attempted to explain, but his mind was made up. The good thing about him was at least he let me know that I was now his enemy. He didn't pretend as if everything was cool and then do things behind my back. No, he made it quite obvious that he was out to get me and reported me to senior management practically every day. He never tried to hide it. Then there was another guy who pretended to have a great relationship with me. I found out later that he had teamed up with the other one and assisted in the slander. Then there were others who thrived off of the rumors the other two had created. It felt more like I was reporting to a zoo rather than a job. That's how wild things had become. I really was dumbfounded. I kept wondering what in the world I was doing wrong. I just couldn't figure it out. I began to communicate heavily with one of my mentors, who at the time was on a six-month prayer mission in Africa. It was he who reminded me that false accusation is the last stage before spiritual promotion.

Let me give you another example. I talked with a friend one evening about this very same topic. Let's call her Ann. I told her that it seemed as if the minute I actually discovered my purpose in life, all hell broke loose. When I say all hell broke loose, that is not an understatement. It seemed like overnight, the people who used to laugh and talk with me began to plot against me. I had done nothing different. I had to realize that it was the enemy at work. Being mindful of who's at work will help you to walk in love and to forgive.

Now back to the story. Ann began to tell me about what she'd recently experienced at work. Everything had been going well during her one year of employment there. She'd never received any sort of reprimand from her supervisor or anything of the sort. She wasn't content with her job because she knew that God was calling her to something greater. Yet she felt as if she could hang in there for a while longer. During this same time period, Ann had been battling with the Lord constantly about what she had been called to do. She knew her calling and had answered it once before. But some things happened in her life that caused her to get temporarily off course. She was ready to make a move but was stuck in that "but how, God?" mode that most of us can relate to. Well, as she began to visualize doing what she loved, an adversary showed up in the form of a new hire. Now, Ann did not know this woman, but it seemed as if there was an instant friction between the two. In a short period of time, Ann became convinced that this young lady had only one mission: to destroy her. The new hire began to make Ann's life a living hell on a daily basis. She made up lies about her and reported her daily to the facility director. Ann worked a 7:00 a.m. to 3:30 p.m. shift. Every day, as she got ready to leave, the new hire would say, "Must be nice to be able to leave early." Ann never responded. When

Ann first started working there, she had to stay as late as 7:00 p.m. and often didn't get off in time to pick up her child from daycare. But over time, she gained a bit of seniority and was able to work more favorable hours.

Ann couldn't figure out what the deal was with this lady. She was obviously doing everything in her power to get Ann fired. Still, she kept quiet. The young lady went on and on. After multiple trips to the director, Ann's shift was changed back to the later one, and guess who got the earlier shift? That's right, the new hire. But that still wasn't enough. The new hire kept lying and complaining until Ann was demoted. The director never once attempted to substantiate any of the claims that had been made against Ann. For some reason, she believed the words of Ann's adversary instead. And that wasn't enough. The girl went on until they finally gave Ann a notice that her hours would be cut. She was now to work four hours a day instead of eight. My friend still kept her mouth shut. She didn't how she would make ends meet. Yet she knew that she was innocent and that God would provide. Sometimes you have to just get downright mad with the devil in order to fulfill your purpose. As a result of the chaos and confusion at work, Ann began to write the plan for her business. She was determined to carry out the vision God had given her this time.

Friend, the moment you discover your assignment, you will also discover your adversary. I'm telling you this so that you will know what to expect and how to prepare—not to deter you from your purpose.

You must know spiritual warfare is real and it is a stepping-stone to promotion. The enemy of your soul will not take your success lying down. He's going to try everything he can to block what God has for you. But he is powerless.

Do you remember what happened to Joseph in the book of Genesis? Let's take a look:

Now Israel loved Joseph more than all his children, because he was the son of his old age: and he made him a coat of many colours. And when his brethren saw that their father loved him more than all his brethren, they hated him, and could not speak peaceably unto him.

(Genesis 37:2–4)

Jacob, who the Lord renamed as Israel, had a total of twelve sons from both of his wives (Rachel and Leah) and from two concubines (Bilhah and Zilpah). You know the story. Jacob, however, plainly loved Rachel more than all of the others, and her son Joseph more than his other sons. This, of course, made Joseph's brothers despise him. As if being the favorite was not enough, Joseph had a dream, that would later be fulfilled in Egypt, that portrayed all of his brothers bowing before him.

And Joseph dreamed a dream, and he told it his brethren: and they hated him yet the more.

*And he said unto them, Hear, I pray you, this dream
which I have dreamed: For, behold, we were binding
sheaves in the field, and, lo, my sheaf arose, and also
stood upright; and, behold, your sheaves stood round
about, and made obeisance to my sheaf.*

(Genesis 37:5–7)

If your baby brother told you that he dreamed you
were bowing down before him, how would you feel?
How would you react? Would you think that he was
crazy and just blow him off or would you react with
pure envy? Perhaps as Joseph's brothers felt, you would
think, *Who is this kid, thinking that he's better than me?*

It didn't end there. Joseph had another prophetic
dream (that would also later be fulfilled in Egypt) in
which he had political power over not only his brothers,
but his father Jacob as well.

*And he dreamed yet another dream, and told it his
brethren, and said, Behold, I have dreamed a dream
more; and, behold, the sun and the moon and the eleven
stars made obeisance to me*

(Genesis 37:9)

At first, Jacob didn't appreciate his son's dreams
any more than Joseph's brothers did, but Jacob, a man
of God who had also experienced prophecies from the
Lord, realized that what was happening was not merely
the idle dreams of a child but the word of God.

71

And he told it to his father, and to his brethren: and his father rebuked him, and said unto him,

What is this dream that thou hast dreamed? Shall I and thy mother and thy brethren indeed come to bow down ourselves to thee to the earth? And his brethren envied him; but his father observed the saying.

(Genesis 37:10–11)

Joseph's brothers became more envious by the second and plotted to kill him. They were tired of him being the favorite and were certainly fed up with the dreams. Instead of killing him, they decided to sell him into slavery. After Joseph was sold into slavery, an Egyptian named Potiphar became his master. Potiphar immediately saw that Jehovah was with Joseph and that Joseph prospered in everything he did. Joseph found favor in Potiphar's sight and was placed as overseer of his house and land. From the time he was made overseer of Potiphar's house and all that he had, the Egyptian's house was blessed for Joseph's sake. Then one day, Potiphar's wife noticed Joseph, for he was a very good-looking man. She approached Joseph and asked him to sleep with her, but he refused. This went on for a while; she approached Joseph daily, and daily Joseph refused. One day she caught Joseph by himself, grabbed him by his clothing, and demanded that he sleep with her. But Joseph ran, instead leaving a piece of garment in her hand. She later showed her husband the piece of garment and told her husband that Joseph tried to rape her. This angered Potiphar. Potiphar took Joseph and placed him in prison. But even in prison, God was with Joseph. He immediately gained favor with the keeper of the prison and was placed in charge of all of the other prisoners.

See a pattern here? Joseph was born to lead. He had a purpose that would be fulfilled no matter the opposition. Friend, so do you. While in prison, Joseph interpreted the dreams of two prisoners: a chief cupbearer and a chief baker. He told the cupbearer that in three days, he would be restored to his office. He told the baker that in three days, he would die. He told the cupbearer to remember him after being released because he had done nothing to be thrown into prison in the first place. But the cupbearer did not remember Joseph. Joseph was in prison, forgotten, for another two years. But God had a purpose in the delay. After all, if God wanted it, the cupbearer could have remembered Joseph a year or more earlier. But God moved in his perfect timing, which is something we often do not understand.

Joseph was not remembered until Pharaoh had a dream that no one else could interpret. It was then that the cupbearer finally remembered Joseph and confessed the wrong he did against him. He recommended Joseph to Pharaoh as a man who interprets dreams. After Joseph interpreted Pharaoh's dream, he then advised him of a plan to handle the famine that would come upon Egypt in seven years.

And the thing was good in the eyes of Pharaoh, and in the eyes of all his servants. And Pharaoh said unto his servants, Can we find such a one as this is, a man in whom the Spirit of God is? And Pharaoh said unto Joseph, Forasmuch as God hath shewed thee all this, there is none so discreet and wise as thou art: Thou shalt be over my house, and according unto thy word shall all my people be ruled: only in the throne will I be greater than thou. And Pharaoh said unto Joseph, See, I have set thee over all the land of Egypt.

(Genesis 41:39–41)

Listen up: during the times when we think God isn't doing anything, he is actually doing the work most important to him. It is during these times that our character is being developed and we are being transformed into the image of his son, Jesus Christ.

Joseph had now gone from the pit to the pinnacle, but it took some thirteen years for it to happen. From the outside, Joseph looked like an immediate success, but it was more than thirteen years in the making. Joseph is a good example of a man who seemed to have all the gifts and talents for leadership, but God developed his character over many years. Gifts and talents may be impressive and immediate, but character is what God looks for and always takes time to develop. Character development is a process that cannot be rushed.

Friend, it may seem as if everyone has forgotten about you; and they may have. They may have forgotten all of your good works and all that you've done for them. It may even seem as if God has forgotten about you. But God will never forget about you. God's will for your life will be accomplished. You too will be pulled out of the pit. Steady your course and allow God to get the glory. False accusations will come. But that's OK. Allow others to mock you while God makes you. Soon all will know that the gracious hand of the Most High God is upon you.

Let us pray:

Father God, you are the God who lifted Joseph up out of the pit and placed him in the palace. You are the same God who answered Elijah by sending fire down from heaven. It is your spirit who lifts up a standard against the enemy when he comes in like a flood. Lord, you are the God who detests lying lips, but takes delight in men who are truthful. It is our prayer now that you will enable us to stand as honest vessels before you. By doing so, we are certain that you will avenge us from our adversaries in Jesus's mighty name. Amen.

CHAPTER TEN

Push Past the Pain

One may go a long way after one is tired.
—French Proverb[1]

God will sometimes create a pain in your life so that you will have no other choice but to seek his face. What do I mean? Often, God allows us to go through things in order to bring us closer to him. It may not make sense at the time, but at some point it will. Just take a moment and reflect back on your life. I am sure that you can a recall a time or two when your back was pushed up against a wall. You couldn't find comfort in anyone else, even though you may have tried. Times like this force us to push back from the everyday hype of life and truly seek God wholeheartedly. It is only after a pushback that we can have a comeback. You will come to a place in your life where you are sick and tired of being sick and tired. You're ready to push.

But the God of all grace, who hath called us unto his eternal glory by Christ Jesus, after that ye have suffered a while, make you perfect, stablish, strengthen, settle you.

(1 Peter 5:10)

God will settle you and perfect all that concerns you, but only after you have been tried and tested. As I've stated time and time again, doing a great work for God is no cakewalk. It will demand so much of you. It may seem as if you are going through trial after trial and test after test. This is no illusion. Yes, you are smack in the middle of the fire of refinement. It may seem as if every time you take a step forward, there is a force trying its best to snatch you backward. One day you're up praising God and thanking him for whatever it is that he has in store for you. The next day, you are crying out to God in despair and asking when the trials will end. Is it really this difficult to answer the call of God? Is it this frustrating? You may ask yourself, "Why does it feel as if I'm in this thing all by myself? Was I even called in the first place?" You may be thinking, *Either I'm dead on it or way off.* You may ask yourself if it's even worth it. Is it worth the sleepless nights? Is it worth being mocked? Is it worth being at the top of the enemy's hit list day in and out? You'll experience so much warfare that you'll just want to tuck your tail and run. But remember:

And let us not be weary in well doing: for in due season we shall reap, if we faint not.

(Galatians 6:9)

You cannot truly understand the magnitude of what God has called you to do. Therefore it will seem very tempting to revert back to your old life. Wouldn't it be easier to just fold? Isn't it something how being in pain can really make you change your mind about things? Listen, this is not the time to swim back to shore; you're in too deep. Too much is on the line. You cannot fold. These feelings are normal, and God knows exactly where you are. I have one word for you: *push*.

When a woman is giving birth, of course she has to push. It is typically a very painful experience. She has to receive instructions about when to push and when to hold in order to prevent distress to her unborn child. So with all of the pushing and pain, she normally cannot tell when the baby is crowning. She has to be prompted by someone skilled on the other end who can actually see what is going on. When the baby crowns, she is very close to delivery, but by this time she is totally exhausted from the demands of labor. So what can she do? She's come too far to give up, so she develops an inner strength and pushes through the pain. The result is the birth of a bouncing baby girl or boy. It has been said that the moment the mother holds her child for the first time, the pain is forgotten. Of course, it hasn't really been forgotten, but the happiness and reward color the memory of the prior pain. This experience is known as the halo effect. So what's the association between childbirth and your assignment?

The pain that you are experiencing can be similar to the agony associated with labor pains. You have been pregnant with something for so long and now the time has come for you to push. You too will want to give up as your purpose crowns, but you can't. You have to trust the one who can see what's going on from the other side: the spirit of God. You must listen to that still-small voice that will tell you when to push and when to hold. Before you know it, you too will have given birth. The moment you are able to hold in your hand what has been in your heart for so long, you too will forget all of the hell that you've gone through to get there.

Remember the story of Hannah? Let's take a look at it:

> Now there was a certain man of Ramathaimzophim, of mount Ephraim, and his name was Elkanah, the son of Jeroham, the son of Elihu, the son of Tohu, the son of Zuph, an Ephrathite: And he had two wives; the name of the one was Hannah, and the name of the other Peninnah: and Peninnah had children, but Hannah had no children. And this man went up out of his city yearly to worship and to sacrifice unto the Lord of hosts in Shiloh. And the two sons of Eli, Hophni and Phinehas,

the priests of the Lord, were there. And
when the time was that Elkanah offered,
he gave to Peninnah his wife, and to all
her sons and her daughters, portions: But
unto Hannah he gave a worthy portion;
for he loved Hannah: but the Lord had
shut up her womb.

(1 Samuel 1–5)

Hannah was married to a man named Elkanah who
dearly loved her, but he also had another wife. The other
wife, Pininnah, had children, but not Hannah. To make
matters worse, Pininnah teased Hannah relentlessly
for her barrenness, causing her great pain. Instead of
retaliating against Pininnah, Hannah decided to seek
God even the more. Remember, it was not the devil
that shut up her womb. It was the Lord: "The Lord had
closed her womb" (1 Samuel 1:5). Hannah continually
sought the Lord to remove her reproach and give her a
male child. She prayed a very powerful prayer in the
first book of Samuel 1:11

And she vowed a vow, and said, O
Lord of hosts, if thou wilt indeed look
on the affliction of thine handmaid,
and remember me, and not forget thine
handmaid, but wilt give unto thine
handmaid a man child, then I will give
him unto the Lord all the days of his

life, and there shall no razor come upon
his head.

After Hannah and her husband Elkanah returned
from Shiloh to their home at Ramah, they slept together.
Scripture says, "And the Lord remembered her" (1
Samuel 1:19). She became pregnant, had a son, and
named him Samuel, which means "God hears."

But remember the promise Hannah made to God?
She promised that if he would give her a male child, she
would lend him back to the Lord all the days of his life.
Hannah followed through on that promise. She handed
her young child Samuel over to Eli for training as a
priest as soon as he was weaned. But it didn't stop there.
God further blessed Hannah for honoring her pledge
to him. She bore three more sons and two daughters.
Samuel grew up to become the last of Israel's judges, its
first prophet, and counselor to its first two kings, Saul
and David.

God created the pain in Hannah's life. Yet it made
her stronger. The position she was placed in forced
her to persevere. Through Hannah's pain, she learned
the power of prayer and persistence. She believed God
when everyone else thought it was impossible. She cried
out to God until she got his attention. At some point,
God noticed her. He looked upon her and blessed her.

Just as the Lord remembered Hannah during her
time of affliction, the Lord will also remember you.
Hannah did not give up because she desired something
so strongly that she couldn't accept no for an answer.

What about you? Will you push past the pain? Will you desire to do the will of God more than anything else? Hannah knew that only God could comfort her. He was the only one who could deliver her. She sought the face of God and was rewarded. The same will happen for you. Prepare yourself, because you ain't seen nothing yet. The reward God has in store for you is so great. Bear down, your water is about to break, and soon you will give life to what you've been carrying all of this time. Get your Kleenex box and keep it close by. Soon all of your tears of pain will turn into tears of joy. Full-scale laughter is in route to you. Receive it in Jesus's name.

Let us pray:

Father God, we thank you for gracing us to carry something so special for your kingdom. You could have chosen anybody but instead you chose us. Lord, we do not take our assignments lightly. Thank you for uniquely tasking us to change the world. We ask you now to guide us by your spirit. We need instruction on how to push past the pain. We know according to your word that we will reap in due season if we faint not. In Jesus's name, we have prayed. Amen.

CHAPTER ELEVEN

The Promise

*Promises, though they be for a time seemingly
delayed, cannot be finally frustrated ... the
heart of God is not turned though His face
be hid; and prayers are not flung back,
though they be not instantly answered.*
—Timothy Cruso[1]

And when Abram was ninety years old
and nine, the Lord appeared to Abram
and said unto him, I am the Almighty
God; walk before me, and be thou
perfect. And I will make my covenant
between me and thee, and will multiply
thee exceedingly. And Abram fell on his
face: and God talked with him, saying,
As for me, behold, my covenant is with
thee, and thou shalt be a father of many
nations. Neither shall thy name any
more be called Abram, but thy name

shall be Abraham; for a father of many nations have I made thee. And I will make thee exceeding fruitful, and I will make nations of thee, and kings shall come out of thee. And I will establish my covenant between me and thee and thy seed after thee in their generations for an everlasting covenant, to be a God unto thee, and to thy seed after thee. And I will give unto thee and to thy seed after thee, the land wherein thou art a stranger, all the land of Canaan, for an everlasting possession; and I will be their God. And God said unto Abraham, Thou shalt keep my covenant therefore, thou, and thy seed after thee in their generations.

(Genesis 17:1–8)

And God said unto Abraham, As for Sarai thy wife, thou shalt not call her name Sarai, but Sarah shall her name be. And I will bless her, and give thee a son also of her: yea, I will bless her, and she shall be a mother of nations; kings of people shall be of her. Then Abraham fell upon his face, and laughed, and said in his heart, Shall a child be born unto him that is an hundred years old? and

shall Sarah, that is ninety years old,
bear?

(Genesis 17:15–17)

This story is a perfect example of how difficult it can sometimes be to accept the promises of God. Abraham actually laughed when God told him that Sarah would give birth to a son in her old age. It seemed ridiculous to believe. We must realize that with God, nothing is impossible. We must also realize that if God said it, he will bring it to pass.

One of the most difficult challenges involved in fulfilling your calling is the removal of your natural reasoning. Now, I'm not saying your head should be up in the clouds, but I am saying you have to stop thinking so much. When God told Abraham that he would be a father to many nations and that Sarah would be a mother to many nations, Abraham immediately assumed that God must've been talking about his son Ishmael. Surely, he couldn't have been referring to a child actually being born to the elderly couple. You know the story. Sarah had been barren for so long that she eventually convinced Abraham to lay with her handmaid Hagar. Together, Abraham and Hagar produced a son named Ishmael. God immediately corrected Abraham and again told him that he and Sarah would indeed have a son and he would be named Isaac. Sure enough, in their old age, they bore a son and named him as instructed.

Now let me ask, how many times has God had to remind you of his promises to you? How many times have you secretly laughed at the thought of what God has called you to do? Is it because it seems to be something too great? Is it because it seems as if you will never get from where you are right now to where God has promised you can be? Was Abraham not filled with doubt when God told him that he and his wife would be the father and mother of many nations? Abraham could not fathom the thought of how this could ever come to pass. Our situations may not be as Abraham's, yet the premise remains. When God declares a thing, it is no longer a laughing matter. It's a truth that will manifest. God is so faithful. I just can't stress it enough. He has promised not to withhold any good thing from you. Why can't we just take God at his word? Why do we continuously allow the enemy to come in and sow seeds of doubt and discouragement? We have to recognize his attacks and cast them down.

Remember the story of Noah building the ark? Was there any rain in sight? No, there wasn't. Yet he had to prepare out of obedience to God. God gave him specific instructions. Noah did not argue with God. He did not put off what he had been chosen to do for a more convenient time. He did not wait for the approval of others. When God told Noah to get moving, Noah obliged. We have to conceptualize the pattern here. All throughout scripture, God has chosen ordinary people to do extraordinary things. Most, if not all, of his instructions made no sense to the natural mind. Does it make sense to march around a wall until it somehow crumbles down? No, but it surely happened.

Did it make sense for Moses to hold out his staff and part the Red Sea? Most certainly not, but it happened. Did it make sense for David to slay Goliath with a sling and a stone? No, it didn't, but he slayed the giant. So why do you think that what God instructs you to do will somehow make sense to your natural mind? Based on God's track record, he just doesn't operate that way. More than likely, there will be very little, if any, physical evidence of how things will work out. You just have to know that regardless of what it looks like right now, heaven will open up and the rain will eventually fall. May God reward you with a torrential downpour of blessings for your faithfulness to his cause.

"And we know that all things work together for good to them that love God, to them who are the called according to his purpose" (Romans 8:28).

When you embrace your purpose, you will embark on an adventure that will last for the rest of your life. When the promises of God begin to manifest as a result of your obedience, you will be amazed. When you close your eyes at the end of your lifetime, you will be able to say, "I made a difference. The world is a better place because of what God called me to contribute." It all boils down to how willing you are to trust God with your life. How willing are you to take God at his word? If he has promised to help you prosper and not harm you, why not believe that? It is his desire for us to prosper. It is God's desire for us to live out our best days now. God is so faithful. He's committed to you. Now you must make the decision to be committed to him and to what he has called you to do. Do not allow distractions from the enemy to cause you to miss the timing of the Lord. He is with you.

The Lord has promised that if you diligently obey his voice, everything that you put your hands to will prosper. Let's look at it in scripture:

> And the Lord shall make thee plenteous in goods, in the fruit of thy body, and in the fruit of thy cattle, and in the fruit of thy ground, in the land which the Lord sware unto thy fathers to give thee. The Lord shall open unto thee his good treasure, the heaven to give the rain unto thy land in his season, and to bless all the work of thine hand: and thou shalt lend unto many nations, and thou shalt not borrow. And the Lord shall make thee the head, and not the tail; and thou shalt be above only, and thou shalt not be beneath; if that thou hearken unto the commandments of the Lord thy God, which I command thee this day, to observe and to do them.
>
> (Deuteronomy 28:11–13)

God loves us so much that he even left simple instructions in his word on how to be successful. The doors to your future are wide open. Please recognize this as your divine time to enter. Remember, to everything there is a season, and a time to every purpose under the heaven (Ecclesiastes 3:3). All that has happened to you up to this point was a part of divine preparation. God was getting you ready for such a time as this. People are waiting on the impact that only you can make. I know that may sound a little hard to believe but it's true.

Let us pray:

Father God, thank you for your many promises. Even when we lost sight, you were right there. Lord, you said that your word will not go out and return void but will do what was intended. Father, we ask you now to do what was intended toward us. Make our lives a wonder to all of those who laughed in our faces. Shock our enemies. Surprise our friends. We'll be careful and we'll be quick to give you all of the glory, honor, and praise that is due unto you. Thank you for choosing us. Great is thy faithfulness! In Jesus's name, we have prayed. Amen.

CHOSEN SCRIPTURES

King James Version

"But ye [are] a chosen generation, a royal priesthood, an holy nation, a peculiar people; that ye should shew forth the praises of him who hath called you out of darkness into his marvellous light." (1 Peter 2:9)

"For thou [art] an holy people unto the LORD thy God, and the LORD hath chosen thee to be a peculiar people unto himself, above all the nations that [are] upon the earth." (Deuteronomy 14:2)

"Blessed [be] the God and Father of our Lord Jesus Christ, who hath blessed us with all spiritual blessings in heavenly [places] in Christ: According as he hath chosen us in him before the foundation of the world, that we should be holy and without blame before him in love." (Ephesians 1:3–4)

"I am crucified with Christ: nevertheless I live; yet not I, but Christ liveth in me: and the life which I now live in the flesh I live by the faith of the Son of God, who loved me, and gave himself for me." (Galatians 2:20)

"And we know that all things work together for good to them that love God, to them who are the called according to [his] purpose." (Romans 8:28)

"Not by works of righteousness which we have done, but according to his mercy he saved us, by the washing of regeneration, and renewing of the Holy Ghost." (Titus 3:5)

"But we are bound to give thanks always to God for you, brethren beloved of the Lord, because God hath from the beginning chosen you to salvation through sanctification of the Spirit and belief of the truth." (2 Thessalonians 2:13)

"Now I tell you before it come, that, when it is come to pass, ye may believe that I am [he]." (John 13:19)

"My Father, which gave [them] me, is greater than all; and no [man] is able to pluck [them] out of my Father's hand." (John 10:29)

"And I appoint unto you a kingdom, as my Father hath appointed unto me." (Luke 22:29)

"And Jesus said unto them, Verily I say unto you, That ye which have followed me, in the regeneration when the Son of man shall sit in the throne of his glory, ye also shall sit upon twelve thrones, judging the twelve tribes of Israel." (Matthew 19:28)

"For I know the thoughts that I think toward you, saith the Lord, thoughts of peace, and not of evil, to give you an expected end." (Jeremiah 29:11)

"For the vision is yet for an appointed time, but at the end it shall speak, and not lie: though it tarry, wait for it; because it will surely come, it will not tarry." (Habakkuk 2:3)

"The Lord will perfect that which concerneth me: thy mercy, O Lord, endureth for ever: forsake not the works of thine own hands." (Psalm 138:8)

"For whom he did foreknow, he also did predestinate to be conformed to the image of his Son, that he might be the firstborn among many brethren." (Romans 8:29)

"I the Lord search the heart, I try the reins, even to give every man according to his ways, and according to the fruit of his doings." (Jeremiah 17:10)

"That which hath been is named already and it is known that it is man: neither may he contend with him that is mightier than he." (Ecclesiastes 6:10)

"Declaring the end from the beginning, and from ancient times the things that are not yet done, saying, My counsel shall stand, and I will do all my pleasure." (Isaiah 46:10)

"Man's goings are of the Lord; how can a man then understand his own way?" (Proverbs 20:24)

"And be not conformed to this world: but be ye transformed by the renewing of your mind, that ye may prove what is that good, and acceptable, and perfect, will of God." (Romans 12:2)

"Commit thy works unto the Lord, and thy thoughts shall be established." (Proverbs 16:3)

"Being confident of this very thing, that he which hath begun a good work in you will perform it until the day of Jesus Christ." (Philippians 1:6)

"And he said unto them, Unto you it is given to know the mystery of the kingdom of God: but unto them that are without, all these things are done in parables." (Mark 4:11)

"Before I formed thee in the belly I knew thee; and before thou camest forth out of the womb I sanctified thee, and I ordained thee a prophet unto the nations." (Jeremiah 1:5)

"For we are his workmanship, created in Christ Jesus unto good works, which God hath before ordained that we should walk in them." (Ephesians 2:10)

"For whosoever will save his life shall lose it: and whosoever will lose his life for my sake shall find it." (Matthew 16:25)

"For thou hast possessed my reins: thou hast covered me in my mother's womb. I will praise thee; for I am fearfully and wonderfully made: marvellous are thy works; and that my soul knoweth right well. My substance was not hid from thee, when I was made in secret, and curiously wrought in the lowest parts of the earth. Thine eyes did see my substance, yet being unperfect; and in thy book all my members were written, which in continuance were fashioned, when as yet there was none of them." (Psalm 139:13–16)

"But as it is written, Eye hath not seen, nor ear heard, neither have entered into the heart of man, the things which God hath prepared for them that love him. But God hath revealed them unto us by his Spirit: for the Spirit searcheth all things, yea, the deep things of God. For what man knoweth the things of a man, save the spirit of man which is in him? even so the things of God knoweth no man, but the Spirit of God. Now we have received, not the spirit of the world, but the spirit which is of God; that we might know the things that are freely given to us of God. Which things also we speak, not in the words which man's wisdom teacheth, but which the Holy Ghost teacheth; comparing spiritual things with spiritual." (1 Corinthians 2:9–13)

NOTES

[1]   Chosen definition: https://www.google.com/search?
q=chosen+definition

Foreword

[1]   Arthur Bennet quote found at http://
www.thirstytheologian.com/2008/07/20/
lords day 29 2008.php (accessed January 15,
2014)

Introduction

[1]   Merriam-Webster.com. Chosen, http://www.
merriam-ictionary/chosen (accessed June 3, 2013).

Chapter One

[1]   Thich Nhat Hanh quote found at Good Reads,http://
www.goodreads.com/quotes/350914-to-be-
beautiful-means-to-be-yourself-you-don-t-need
(accessed June 1, 2013)

Chapter Two

[1] Publilius Syrus quote found at Life Hack, http://quotes.lifehack.org/quote/publilius-syrus/how-unhappy-is-he-who-cannot-forgive/ (accessed June 1, 2013)

[2] Agave Americana, Wikipedia, http://en.wikipedia.org/wiki/Agave_americana (accessed July 5, 2013).

Chapter Three

[1] John F. Kennedy quote found at http://www.presidency.ucsb.edu/ws/?pid=74076 (accessed June 15, 2013).

Chapter Four

[1] Mike Huckabee quote found at Liberty vs Tyranny, http://liberty-vs-tyranny.com/Mike-Huckabee-Quotes.htm(accessed June 15, 2013)

Chapter Five

[1] John Pemberton, Wikipedia, http://en.wikipedia.org/wiki/John_Pemberton (accessed September 5, 2013).

Chapter Six

[1] Albert Einstein quote found at Wikiquote, http://en.wikiquote.org/wiki/Talk:Albert_Einstein (accessed on July 1, 2013).

[2] "26 People who failed first" Business Insider, accessed on July 15, 2013, http://www.businessinsider.com/26-successful-people-who-failed-at-first-2012-7?op=1

[3] John Kennedy Toole, Wikipedia, http://en.wikipedia.org/wiki/John_Kennedy_Toole, accessed on August 1, 2013

Chapter Seven

[1] Jonathan Edwards quote found at Graphepress, http://site.graphepress.com/viewpagescharity.htm (accessed on July 31, 2013).

Chapter Eight

[1] T.S.Eliot quote found at Goodreads, http://www.goodreads.com/author/quotes/18540.T_S_Eliot (accessed on July 10, 2013).

[2] Nik Willenda, CBS News, http://www.cbsnews.com/8301-201_162-57590613/daredevil-nik-wallenda-trying-to-cross-gorge-near-grand-canyon/ (accessed August 15, 2013)

Chapter Nine

[1]   Mike Murdock Quote found at Jerry A Chadwick, http://www.jerryachadwick.com/article_7.html (accessed on August 1, 2013)

Chapter Ten

[1]   French Proverb Quote found at Quotes Valley, http://www.quotesvalley.com/one-may-go-a-long-way-after-one-is-tired-french-proverb/ (accessed October 15, 2013)

Chapter Eleven

[1]   Timothy Cruso quote found at Spurgeongems, http://www.spurgeongems.org/iquotes.htm#Love (accessed on November 1, 2013)

ABOUT THE AUTHOR

Dr. Kellie Lane is a family nurse practitioner, motivational speaker, life coach, and author. She has dedicated her life to empowering others to reach their maximum potential in Christ. Coining the phrase "push, pray, and persist," Lane encourages her readers to stop whining and complaining, get up, and do. She says, "Expect challenges along the way, but don't let that stop you. Don't look at your obstacles as hindrances; view them as opportunities." Lane says it all boils down to how bad you want it. *Chosen* is her second astounding work, tailing her first success, *When God Is Silent*. She again takes the reader on a spiritual journey that leads to a deeper revelation and tender love for the omnipotent Almighty God. According to Dr. Lane, nothing that you go through in life is in vain. All of it, the good, the bad, and the ugly, sculpts you into the fine art you were predestined to become. She charges every reader to go get God's best.

Dr. Lane is a happily married mother of six. She resides in Jackson, Mississippi.

//P

9 781496 918925